C.D. Hurley

Squirrels And Quasars & Stuff

Prose and Poetry

RED LEAD PRESS
PITTSBURGH, PENNSYLVANIA 15222

ISBN-978-0-8059-8365-4
Library of Congress Control Number: 2006932108
Printed in the United States of America

First Printing

For more information or to order additional books, please contact:
Red Lead Press
701 Smithfield Street
Third Floor
Pittsburgh, Pennsylvania 15222
U.S.A.
1-800-834-1803
www.redleadbooks.com

My appreciation to:

Granddaughter ROXANNE MARIE McGAFFIGAN
for visiting my childhood homeland with me,
and for suggesting that I write my stories,

and to:

My friend and editor, FREDERICKA TAPPAN
for her tireless editing and endless encouragement,

THANK YOU!
C.D. Hurley

This book is dedicated to

WILLIAM MICHAEL MCGAFFIGAN

SQUIRRELS And QUASARS & Stuff
PROSE AND POETRY

ADDED FOR YOUR ENJOYMENT,

BOOK BONUS #1 A CHRONICLE OF TRUE SHORT STORIES

and

BOOK BONUS #2 MUSE SEASON

By: C.D. Hurley

Contents

That Squirrel in My Backyard

That little gray squirrel, in my back yard, just who does he think he is
sitting out in the open lawn, an easy prey for me?
He looks out over his kingdom, sometimes looking straight at me,
forcing my mind to question, "Just who is the dominate one?"

Now, if I can just open this storm door a little bit, Ole Chloe will run him down
and chew him up, starting with that tail. That'll teach him a thing or two!
But Chloe wouldn't swallow him,
'cause she only eats "Little Nuggets" from the store
and I don't think, with the fur and all, squirrel would taste that good.

The handle to the door is up so high that I can't even open it,
and Chloe is standing on her tiptoes, but she still can't reach that high.
If I pick her up, I'll need both hands to lift her enough to reach it
then I can't open the door, 'cause I only have two hands.

Up and down that live oak tree, he climbs and hangs and glides
and his friends show up and play their games of "squirrel" hide and seek.
Then he looks around and scratches his belly
that looks like it's made of cotton,
then it's back up the tree to his playmates,
and the game starts all over again.

Yes, I remember back, when I was that age, so many years ago.
I never, ever, could even come close to catching that little gray squirrel
but Chloe did; well she came close, but never really succeeded.
Then, as we got older, we both just lost all interest in it, I guess.

I'm glad we didn't catch that little gray squirrel,
nor teach him a thing or two,
and "my Chloe" has gone to Heaven,
where I know she'll be waiting for me.
I'll bet that scene is repeated on a million different mornings.
I hope those million memories will remain as sweet as mine.

My Great Smoky Mountain Home

I'm standing alone on this mountaintop, looking as far as I can see.
Each mountain seems to be farther away, as it hides in its smoke-like screen
until the last one I see, or I think that I do, seems to be just barely defined,
I think, "Do I see it? Is it really there? Do I trust my eyes or my mind?"

The closest mountain appears to me as though, by traveling for a day,
I can be where the smoke stands sentry, nearly hiding her away.
And the third wears a veil so unrevealing,
it seems my journey would be so impaired
that perhaps it would take a lifetime for me, just to travel there.

But if I leave my mountain to go there and find that I cannot return,
this then would become the third mountain and,
even though I would yearn,
I could never come back to my mountain, no matter how much I may long.
So, I think I'll just stay here forever, in my Great Smoky Mountain Home.

Love Story

I was born to a loving family where smiles were "the uniform of the day".
I could sing and yell to my hearts content and no one would drive me away.
I ran barefoot through fields of sunshine and clear, clean, country air.
My problems were all solved for me then, so I never had a care.

I had freedom of thought and freedom of mind and never was I restricted.
As I grew into a young man, those freedoms were not affected.
I became an infantry soldier and soon met the girl of my dreams.
She became mother of my children and we made a great family team.

We traveled often around the country teaching flight to military cadets,
and moved often from one base to another
as "the needs of the service" were met.
Then finally, we stopped the moving and stayed for a time in one berth,
meeting many wonderful people, from all around the earth..

I began a career as pilot, on a schedule; so now we could plan.
I saw the world from high aloft and in wonderment, again and again.
Our children grew up and grandchildren came, two each, boys and girls,
and soon, behold great-grandchildren. We explored a brand new world.

Yes, our "life's song" was being played again,
with individuals from within our "clan".
The girls became perfect ladies and the boys, dashing young men.
Marie and I just sat and watched as the future paraded by.
We watched our life repeat itself right before our eyes.

Now, I can see, my hands have grown old, and Marie has a few gray hairs.
I look into her eyes and see she is tired, but her sparkle lingers there.
There's a smile for the good life we've had together,
with a bit, still left to go.
I take her hand and kiss her palm. She just smiles, then whispers, "I know!"

Where I Grew Up

Where I grew up on a Dixie farm, most always, it was summertime.
Cut- off pants was all I wore, clothes were never on my mind.
Cedars were all called Christmas trees and daffodils were Easter flowers.
Church was held in the Shady Grove schoolhouse
and the rains were mostly showers.

In May, the last school days were held. It was a joyous time of year.
I think everyone passed in that one-room school.
We were each other's peers.
We were free to do what suited us, after we accomplished our chores,
but when they were done, we could roam at will and daydream and explore.

Woods and caves and ponds and lakes were all just waiting for me
to climb and swim and throw a stone,
with trips just to find what I could see.
Mountain clean air and a bright blue sky;
I drank water from a cold, clear stream.
Sometimes my father would let me help by driving his two-horse team.

The wheat threshers came with all the hands to feast on my mother's meals
and thresh the golden fields of grain between the soft green hills.
The fourth of July was to celebrate, and celebrate we did.
The day, always a celebration for us, was spent with the community's kids.

We helped with the planting and harvest, preparing the family's food.
We plucked and hoed and gathered corn and chopped and stacked the wood.
But soon, new clothing was purchased and September came around again.
A new school year was started and a higher grade began.

But we still had some harvesting to do and we gathered for molasses stirs,
ice cream suppers and cakewalks, where boys and girls were paired.
And sometimes the preacher came home with us to take his Sunday meal
of fried chicken, and upside down cake, served in an open field.

We soon said "adieu" to that old school, the new in another town.
Some folks went east and some went west, we kids scattered all around.

Some left the area; I went away to serve my nation's call.
I lost track of the kids from the old school, but I still remember them all.

Sometimes, I see a familiar name that reached a milestone of some type,
but then, our getting older makes those milestones mostly hype.
Those accomplishments usually mean nothing;
my memories now mean more.
We passed our greatest milestones, I think,
at that school near the country store.

I just wonder sometimes if we may be making some very big mistakes.
Our lifetime of accomplishments is touted, during or just after our wakes,
but I credit my start on the better life to the gift that molded my ways.
That one- room school in the church house,
and my memories of yesterday.

Into Your Arms Again

Let me come into your arms again,
that is where I long to be again.
There your softness comforts me, and puts my heart and mind at ease,
take me back within your arms again.

As I wake to face the world alone
without you, I must continue on.
My life seems to just stand still, without your love I have no will,
'til I'm safe within your arms again

Soon, I hope to make it home to you.
My duty served and then my work is through.
I'll rush home to hold you tight, through the day and through the night,
so in love, within your arms again.

I know, it's been a long, long time.
and I promise you a life, so fine.
Just hold me close and tell me true that there is no one else for you,
and take me home, within your arms again.

One Time

One time,
in the midst of our youth, you and I first met,
and explored our thoughts, so sweet and free.
We yearned for each other and fell in love,
one time.

And one time,
we were never alone, and we would never stray.
We needed each other and could never part.
Our plans were echoes of the other's thoughts,
one time

And one time,
on a Sunday in June, we said "I do!"
The world was all flowers, the bright sun shone
We took each forever; our love could never change,
one time.

And one time
my contentment was in your happiness,
and I thought that surely you would always love me,
but I didn't have answers for the right thing to do,
one time!

And one time,
a judge said that you should raise all of our kids.
I was not to be seen near you again.
Our world slipped away from us. It took all our dreams
one time.

Now, this last time
Sweetheart, I beg this favor of you.
Know my heart is breaking, as inside I cry,
and I ask your forgiveness as I say goodbye
this last time.

Ocean Reunion

Walking together again, on our favorite shoreline,
my memories to share, just with you,
of building a life for our children
and even a great grandchild or two.

Take a look through my glasses to where the sky clashes
and see the turmoil the sea is going through.
It's a symbol of our love life, My Darling,
the story of me and of you.

We were so young and we were both filled with hope,
our ambitions were as wide as the sea.
Then, as deep and as calming as ocean water in summer,
your love just washed over me.

Our love was as wide as this ocean you see,
and I floated in my deepest dreams.
Then our ocean fell dry of love and we parted.
Our future had ended, it seemed.

Now we walk here again, still deeply in love?
Can we live in our glory again?
But now, in the twilight of our being,
walk slow Love, and hold my wrinkled hand.

I need you to talk to and to share all our memories,
I need you to care about me,
while remembering the joys of two lovers
in their youth, in the sand, by the sea.

Life s Trepan

I was.
We were.
I am.
You will be.
Yes! Someday we all shall be.

A Story on the TV News

I was watching news of a war in a land far, far away.
A people were rounded up in herds and driven to the beach to die.
Men and women and children, no mercy to any would befall.
They waited for their penalty; death would be delivered to all

A young lady stood by the waters crying, tears dripping off her pretty nose.
Her mouth was opened in anguish, her small young hands clasped closed.
While a companion reflected her hopelessness, pain engraved in his face,
they waited for death by an army whose orders were to eradicate their race.

What happened next was far too graphic for an audience to see
So the picture was continued later from a point along the beach.
All was quiet, there were no more tears.
There were bodies scattered near and far.
I thought; "the devil may have won the battle but,
the Lord will win that war".

I cried! And the memory of the children's faces would never let me rest.
They had no one to turn to, no one to listen
and they knew they would experience death.
They were so alone, so stricken with fright and I could only pray
that my grandchild was safe and asleep in her bed,
tired from too much play.

I prayed that the children died quickly, enduring no more fright or pain,
and for Jesus to take them to his side, for eternity to remain.
Free of suffering from enemies forever, to know agony no more.
In the Lord's House, there are no battles, only peace.
Yes, the children will have won the war.

Ocean Sail

WHOOOOOOOOOOSHeeeeeeeeeeeeeeeeeeeeeeeeeeeeeeeeeeeeeeeeeee!
The foaming blue-green waters slide across the golden sand
gradually losing its power and gliding back to await another surge.
WHOOOOOOOOOOSHeeeeeeeeeeeeeeeeeeeeeeeeeeeeeeeeeeeeeeeeeee!
Seabirds race to find a tiny bit of food and run away from the next wave.
There is no break and no rest period,
just a continuous washing of the sands of the beach.
WHOOOOOOOOOOSHeeeeeeeeeeeeeeeeeeeeeeeeeeeeeeeeeeeeeeeeeee!
Walking barefoot to the dock, I carry my shoes over my shoulders.

My sailboat waits in her tether,
barely feeling the waves breaking on her bow.
I board, stowing my shoes below for a later time.
I check her stores for the necessities for her care and use.
I check my stores for the necessities for me.

Her sails are furled and her beam is shackled to a dockside piling.
I free her life's moor now as surely as I free mine,
From the ties that are safe from the whim of the ocean's spirit,
we now present our souls and body to her choice of wrath or care.

With a gentle shove, I sever our ties with the world we knew.
With the slithering sounds of the surf in the background, still.
I set her sails to catch the breeze that comes from somewhere offshore
to replace the air displaced by the heating sun.

The slapping waves are tamed to a soft stroke by my sailboat's bow,
cutting smooth and effortless through deeper waters as we sail away.
Away from the shore that tied us to life's countless things,
and now, there are three; the ocean, my sailboat, and me.

Just three, of all God's subjects, are as one again.
Each one is a servant to the other and each to Him.
My boat to me and I to it and the sea is there to caress us.
I pray to Him to make my sail complete.

Clambake

On a cool September afternoon, I was on my way to Maine,
making a very enjoyable trip in marking another year.
Too early for the colorful leaves yet, the sky was crystal clear
I'm meeting with my fellow workers, called Northeast Yellowbirds.

I arrived there nice and early, with time to look around.
Souvenirs that cost a dollar this summer, marked down to fifty cents.
Cohorts started showing slowly, donning jackets for the cold,
Still holding out, in my short sleeve shirt, I think, "They are getting old."

I worry that I won't know the people that I will be meeting inside,
but that thought is soon forgotten,
replaced with new friendships and smiles.
Strangers stepped up and greeted
anyone who may have been standing alone,
and the hall had filled with the music of laughter, in just a little while

Conversations were of old days, things we did "way back when",
sharing stories half remembered, needing help to get "filled in"
Secretaries, agents, mechanics, pilots, worked in flight and on the ground.
All did their part for a proficient airline, moving passengers around.

I met one, and then another old acquaintance from another time.
Even strangers became familiar in this reunion from the old airline.
We conversed and shared a meal together; none were strangers any more.
Soon, the hall became much quieter as guests drifted out the door.

"Well, here's 'till next year then, old friend, don't forget to call or write!
Let me know how you make out now, you going back south tonight?"
As I struggle to my auto, I notice more of us are walking slow.
I'm reminded that our ranks are thinning,
next year some will be "no-shows"

I sit a moment and then call my wife, to check on how she feels
and to tell her, I have a lobster dinner for her and, not to take a meal.
Then I start my homeward journey, while I try to remember the words
to the tune that was once the theme song of the Northeast Yellowbirds.

Spring s Alarm

Nature's inner alarm clock rings,
heralding the start of an early spring.
Makes the mouth curl high in back,
up to the ears and back to the neck.
Winter's cold is foiled again.
Life is grand, so let the good times begin

Look Up

When you begin to feel you have lost the race, look up,
and see His face.
When loneliness starts to make you cry, look up,
and see His sky.
When heartbreak's more than you can bear, look up,
and see Him there.
"When it's time to leave this world", says He,
"Lift up thine eyes, and come to Me!"

Blow On, North Wind

Blow on, North wind!
Your lonesome sounds and your biting cold
make my mind and body know
that I must hide away in my comforts,
knowing, and in spite of you.

My mind's at ease!
I think of life in personal terms
of my relationships in another time,
as I lie here in my solitude,
and hear your lonesome song.

I'll sleep tonight!
My mind recalls its mortal joys
while you invoke your cries of noise.
I'll close my eyes and remember,
and yes, perhaps I'll dream.

As I lie down,
I offer up my daily prayers.
While songs emanating from your icy lair
threaten my bones with winter chill.
I'll light a fire, and rest.

Blow on, North wind!
I hear your howl, and feel your pain
as winter's long, hard grip remains
to keep you in close abeyance,
As I sleep. as I sleep!

Seastorm

My stately ship begins our journey on a sullen sea
amidst our hopes for a friendly ‘n favorable wind.
There’s many a mile o’ sea t’ sail before us,
‘n many a day t’ sail ‘fore our journey’s through.

Away from shore for a fortnight, ‘n the stars are hiding in the heavens.
Oh God! Our faith’s with You that Your Sea will soon be stilled.
Satan rides the waves ‘n stirs the seas wild in our path of travel,
whipping the frenzied sea froth high in ‘is deadly brew.

The curse o’ stormy sea ‘n devil winds a-blow
hang powerful upon my ship tonight
and the scourge o’ sickness weighs heavily on ‘er captain’s hand.
Do I hear, in the winds, the sound of Gabriel’s Horn a-blowing for me?
Pray that I not take my flight encrusted by the salty sea.

My ship shudders in ‘er fight against an angry ocean storm
that plays with ‘er courage, as if awaiting the proper time t’ kill.
‘Er bow is held Heavenward by a giant crest o’ water.
Last chance for prayer; she’s now at the altar’s edge.

Its grip released as if for bad food, turned away.
‘Er bow falls helpless down toward a silent grave.
The sounds of the ocean closing heavy down upon ‘er
as my ship stops fighting; trembling in the jaws o’ death.

“Er timbers cry from the burden o’ the ocean’s might upon ‘er
like the sounds o’ man emitting the final throes o’ death,
yet, ‘er heart still lives. I know not how she fights so gallantly.
Then, with one violent thrust, she trembles from ‘er bowels t’ ‘er stem.

She thrusts ‘er bow upward again toward Heaven
as if t’ clear ‘er conscience of ‘er duties t’ earth ‘n man.
Prostrating her blooded body on the ocean’s deadly altar,
the battle’s over; my ship gives up ‘er long ‘n courageous fight.

But, alas! The Angels have regained control o'er the wicked devil's seas.
My ship now rests as 'er storm sails 'r struck, and 'er mainsails fly.
She regains 'er course, 'n yes, regains 'er dignity.
She proudly plies the ocean, with a steady course, again.

"Oh, mighty ship, that fought the angry seas so gallantly,
little less than God doth thy sweet soul mean t' me.
T'would be my honor t' guide your path 'n t' serve as your Master, forever.
God give me the wit 'n skill t' guide all your passages."
AMEN!
Your Humble Captain.

There Is Something Different About You

The way you looked at me when I first saw you,
the way you smiled when we were first introduced,
the way you held your head, when you made a statement.
There was definitely something different about you

The way you walked, after your mind was made up,
the way you came to me and let me hold your hand,
the way we could talk so easily together.
There was definitely something different about you.

The way you looked at me from across the dance floor,
the way we conversed, right through a crowd,
the way you kissed me when I said "I love you!".
There was definitely something different about you.

The way we laughed when we were together,
the way you walked with joy on the sandy beach,
The look in your eyes when I said, "forever".
There was definitely something different about you.

The way we raised and cherished our children,
the way I knew I could depend on you,
the way we loved and the memories you left me.
There was definitely something different about you.

You are in my heart and in my dreams forever.
You are in my memories, every day of my life.
There are a million reasons why I'll love you forever,
There is definitely something different about you.

Beowulf Gypsia
(Charlie)

We were all smiles as we brought home a tiny German Shepherd pup
with leashes and harness, dishes and blankets, we even had a gate
to keep our doggie safe and warm to sleep the winter nights away.
That's what we planned, but we soon learned,
that our puppy would always be up.

We named him Beowulf for his dad and Gypsia for his mom.
He ate with us, played in our bed, then slept a big part of the day.
We made no noise, lest we wake him again, and ruin his beauty sleep.
His new Mom and Dad got very little rest,
watching over their adopted son.

But, the "little puppy" time was to be short-lived,
and soon he attended school,
To learn discipline, walk, and obey me and to come when he was called.
He learned his lessons fast and complete, and soon was released.
Before he came home, I attended class to learn his handler's rules.

I had bragged too much about my puppy's progress
and how he knew his commands.
I was showing him off to a friend of mine, when he suddenly ran away.
He had a great time running through town, with me trailing behind.
When his game had ended, I promised him sternly
that he wouldn't escape again

He was a brilliant companion, and obedient beyond compare.
I fell in love with "Charlie" as we grew together day by day.
He loved all types of creatures and people, especially little ones.
He made many friends, as he accompanied his master to almost anywhere.

Rides in the truck, walks in the woods, and sometimes an ice cream cone
was enjoyed by the family, along with Charlie, most any flavor would do.
Once he found an abandoned raccoon, which we brought home and raised
To become a mother of many fine cubs until she finally left our home.

As I walked in the woods, he ran circles around me,
making noise while rustling leaves.
If I stopped walking, he would stop running,
and listen to see where I had gone.
When I moved again, he would resume his play
and eventually come to me.
Then, we would sit in the sun, with his head in my lap,
and often, we would fall asleep.

As the years passed us by his gait slowed down,
and he would bypass the stairs
and slowly walk up the hill to the front door, where I would help him in.
He would sleep for longer and longer periods,
and I knew the day would soon be at hand,
when his vet would advise me to end his pain,
and administer the ultimate care.

That day came too soon and early one morning, his vet stood at the door
beside Charlie's bed where I held him, stroking his silver-black coat.
He said, "My friend, the time has come to put your dog to rest."
I know Charlie knew what he was saying as he lay in his bed on the floor.

Suddenly, Charlie stood up,
walked to his dish and took in a long, cool drink.
Then he walked back to me,
and I picked him up and carried him out to the lawn.
I sat down in the grass and kissed his face
and I told my best friend "goodbye".
Mark administered the shot and he was gone before I had time to think.

I carried his body to the car, where I kissed him and Mark drove away.
My heart turned into hot jelly, it seemed,
and I dropped to the ground in tears.
Just like that, my world was over. I can't compare the pain.
I will never forget my friend Charlie. I miss him more every day.

It has been many years since my best friend died
and I dream of him often, still.
I dream I see him lying down and run to him, but he moves away,
Then, when I awake, sometimes I cry. I'm not over losing him.
He taught me so much. Now, I am the one who slowly walks up that hill.

When My Maker calls me and I go to heaven, as soon as I process in,
I will meet with my family, my Dad and my Mother
and look all around The Throne
'til I find my pal Charlie, I know he'll be waiting,
and we'll go for a long, long run.
On the day I arrive there, with my broken heart repaired,
we'll let the Great Reunion begin.

Rain on the Window

The rain, running down the windowpane,
brings memories of nights that wouldn't last,
reminds me of the life we shared together,
and leaves me smiling for the good times of our past.

My heart aches because I cannot touch you.
My tears fall from the sorrow I feel inside,
and wash away all hope for my tomorrows.
I am left with an emptiness by my side.

If I could have just one wish tonight dear,
it would be to hold you close to me once again,
while you assure me softly of our enduring love,
as the rain runs down the windowpane

Across the Mountain

There's a wonderful place nestled at the north foot of the Cumberland Mountain Range where I lived when I was a little boy.
Long ago, my family moved from that magical place, to just over the other side of the mountain, to another farm.
Often, because much of the family was left in the first domain, Mother would tell us to "Get ready! We are 'going across the mountain'".

That phrase always meant going to the place where we were born. We were returning to the place my family called home.
We were going back to the family roots, where our ancestors lie in their final resting places and where my parents, their parents, and their parents were born.
Of all seven children, I don't remember one who wanted to stay at home when the family was "going across the mountain".

Seven children and Mom and Dad squeezed into the little "Model 'A'" Ford. I stood behind the front seat, in the middle, behind my sister.
I never sat, so I could watch how beautifully my father handled those hair-pin curves, gearing down and up flawlessly until we reached our first stop.
A reed carried ice-cold water from the mountain rocks. Dippers, made from gourds, were left for travelers and as we drank and rested, we enjoyed the view.

The trip down the other side presented its own problems, I could not see the sky, only moving trees, which caused my stomach to become upset.
My precious mother gave me spearmint gum to occupy my mind but, mixed with travel sickness, it only caused me to despise the flavor.
Soon however, we arrived at the place we called home, Yellow Branch Church. The surrounding mountains and rolling hills had been branded into our being.

Someone, either friend or relative, always had a meal and a "spring-cooled" drink to share with us and laughter soon began.
A bond existed among the families who were always there to help or lend a hand in any crisis, no matter how small or how large.
We sometimes would visit the gravesites of our ancestors,

family members who had gone to their final rest before us.

We played “red rover” and “tag” and “hide and seek”
and newly discovered wonders were shared with us.
We often would stop playing to sit and listen
to the grown-ups tell their wonderful stories
of the “olden times”, and how they had overcome adversities.
We learned that humor can come from hard times spent together.
Love, companionship and humor were sometimes all they had.

It always seemed that the day had just begun when Dad signaled that we
must be leaving, before the setting sun transformed
the mountain shadows to darkness.
The cows would be waiting, no matter if we were late or early, but Dad
always kept the time of milking the same each day,
So we would start our journey home and my baby sister and I,
tired and comfortable, soon fell asleep.

On arrival home, our chores awaited us, and we were always treated to a
hot meal, after which we would fall asleep
while re-living our day in conversation and thoughts.
Tomorrow, we would find our routine again
and do the things families do together to survive as such.
We would work, and go to church, laugh and sing. We would all re-seal
our bond as a family and eagerly await Mom’s call to
“Clean up! We’re ‘going across the mountain’!”

A New Swimmin Hole

Searching for adventure in the woods,
we find a pond, with lots of mud.
We run and jump in on a dare,
indifferent to what could be waiting there

We laugh and dive in the yellow muck.
(If we don't die it will be by luck.)
Old cottonmouth is hidden away
waiting to bite us another day

We wait around for our pants to dry,
donning nothing for a while.
Then, wearing them home while they are still wet,
we end the day with the best swimming yet!

Mom doesn't notice and I don't volunteer,
she surely would throw me outta' here.
Hope her chair will be dry when supper's done.
I eat and leave the table on the run.

I pretend to be sleeping when Mom comes in.
I'm waiting for my whippin' to begin
but she kisses me and says "Goodnight!"
I'm thanking My God for my Mom tonight.

Northeast Yellowbirds

Working for the Air Force as a Flying Instructor,
I was as happy as could be,
when the Pentagon, suddenly cut the Air Force's budget,
thereby, displacing me.
I was offered the same instructing job, but at another base,
a place that I didn't care for, so I began to wait.

I soon received a telephone call from an airline Vice-President.
He asked me to come to see him in Boston, and eventually, I went.
He needed help in training new pilots; new-hires, they were called.
After weeks of discussions, I agreed to the job,
with better benefits, wages and all.

But very soon, I began to dislike this new position I was in,
being groomed for the position of Director of Training,
where I would begin
managing the company's Ground School Instructors,
whom I had never met.
I decided that I wished to leave the position that I hadn't even started yet.

The Vice-President asked what he could offer to convince me to stay.
I answered, "A pilot seniority number!" He answered "Not right away!"
"On the first working day of next month", he said, "I'll put you on the list,
however, you will stay, as a ground instructor, until you are dismissed".

During my year in the Training Department,
I made many new acquaintances
from the flight crews, and executive officers,
to the people in aircraft maintenance.
I met dispatchers, planners, and crew schedulers,
reservationists and even clerks,
and hundreds of other specialists that make a great airline work.

In the spring of 1967, I would learn to fly the new Fairchild
and be assigned to the airline's New York Base, for a just a little while,
I was injured in a bout with turbulence; a gust that was so strong

that my seatbelt snapped, I received a concussion,
and the doctors sent me home

I was grounded for a month, but when that passed, I was eager to fly again.
With the Flight Surgeon's release,
I returned to "the line", to start all over again.
I flew to Rockland, Bar Harbor, Berlin, Keene, Montpelier and more.
New people and places that were so beautiful, it made my spirits soar.

Then after a year flying the Fairchild, I trained for the DC-9,
a pure jet so sophisticated and fun, I would stay for a long, long time.
Then I changed my seat to the Captain's chair,
and continued to love every minute.
My love of those crews and that aircraft made it
a difficult decision to leave it.

But finally, after twelve years of flying the "9", I changed to the "727",
A move I questioned greatly at first, but soon she became "my heaven".
She would do anything I asked of her,
and was scheduled for the longer "runs".
With an engineer to help with the cockpit chores, she sure was a lot of fun.

There were days of sweet rapture, days of joy, and days of total bliss.
But there were also some days where I worked hard,
and days I had trouble with.
There was one "rotation" that I reported for the first flight, at 1 AM,
with an early morning arrival in New Orleans in fog,
with the sunlight beaming in.

I would try to sleep, with no "blackout shades",
and with jackhammers on the street.
I wound up sleeping in an all day movie;
returning to the airport was a treat.
In the early evening I was off again to other exotic places.
I would keep this up for four days, returning home to collect all the pieces.

But the bulk of my journey in my airline career,
brought pride, and a lot of joy
in working with people who were always trying
to make life better than before.
In all the years that I worked there, no one would give me pause.
Everyone I worked with was a professional in their position,
no matter what it was.

Now I've grown old and have been retired for over twenty years.
And I look back to my memories and come close to shedding tears
for the profession I had, the people I met,
and fellow workers who have touched
my life in the journey. They made it much better;
I miss them all very much.

I travel when I can, but when I do; it just doesn't seem the same.
The people are different, so are the airplanes,
even the new paint scheme is strange.
So I'll sit at my p/c and fall asleep while putting memories into words.
Of those wonderful days and those wonderful people,
"The Northeast Yellowbirds".

Now, with my great-grandchildren, I tell them stories of people I know,
and the tales that are funny or tales of the cities
where Great-Grandpa got to go.
We'll play hide and seek, and go for a walk,
or just sit and learn some new words.
I'll be wearing my mask of "The Big Green Gorilla",
with the heart of a Yellowbird.

Airliner

She is taxied into position, and awaits the "Clear to go!"
The pilot advances the fuel levers and the engines start to roar.
The brakes are released, power is checked, airspeed starts to build.
At the proper time, her nose is rotated and the earth loses its grip.

She smoothly climbs into her realm, where she was created to be,
where an aircraft reigns in its own domain in the atmosphere, alive and free.
Her engines power her through the air and her character starts to show.
It's something that only a pilot can feel, yes, only her pilot knows.

He guides her across the surface of air. Faster and faster she flies.
Upward and onward her grace is displayed, lifting herself to the skies,
'til she's sliding beneath the cumulus clouds, and causing them to spin.
Her powerful wings make their presence known; the aircraft is at home again.

The clouds soon are left to the world below; she flies where the sky is clear.
She has reached the cold crystal of the edge of space;
jet aircraft are comfortable here.
No eagle has ever flown in this realm;
few objects have reached these heights.
Then the power is set 'til the engines relax,
disguising the sound of their might.

The earth moves slowly beneath her as her wings are trimmed to full sail.
Her engines mark the blue of the autumn sky
with a brilliant white contrail.
The plane and her pilot both relax in the frozen ionosphere.
Her descent is delayed to the last moment,
as the optimum conditions are here.

Although she belongs, it won't be long before alas, her nose is lowered.
She starts her descent toward a runway, almost a hundred miles forward,
and a half dozen miles below her. Now she enters the atmosphere
and meets her counterparts departing and arriving from everywhere.

She is slowed and dressed for a landing, her gear is lowered down,
her wings are adjusted for maximum lift
as her flight path nears the ground.
The pilot flares her for touchdown and a smooth landing on the runway.
She will now be pampered with supplies and fuel,
then continue her busy day.

That's a portion of a day in an aircraft's life, of going from place to place,
from the busy airport atmosphere to the edge of outer space,
taking cargo and people from every country, to any place on earth,
transporting them quickly, in comfort and safety, for better or for worse

Since 1903, in Kitty Hawk, aircraft have fascinated man
with flight, for business and for pleasure, at speeds we can't understand.
They move their cargo from place to place,
and this earth just isn't the same
as it was before the Wright brothers flew
the first of those wonderful airplanes.

The Fly-In

I woke up early this fall morning, eager to start my day,
a trip to the bank and post office, and then I was on my way,
to pick up Freddie in Windham, for a drive up Route 93.
We'll arrive in Tilton in an hour or so, and then we'll get something to eat.

Then our next stop will be Plymouth Airport,
where we'll find many people we met
while working together in the airline business,
most retired, some are working yet!
We arrived at the field to warm sunshine; early fog had burned away.
Some planes were starting to land on the grass;
it looked like a wonderful day.

There were private planes and motorcycles from near, and some from far,
and one arrival by farm tractor, but most arrived by car.
We talked and remarked "You're looking great" to everyone we see.
It feels good to see my old friends. Hope they're happy to see me.

There were tales and plenty of laughter,
and our memories seemed to be fine.
Some happenings seemed like yesterday and others a long, long time.
It's good to spend time with my old friends; it's good to talk with them
but there are more and more that are missing, some won't return again.

We can only count our blessings, that today we could meet again
and soon, too soon, its time to go to our homes, "around the bend".
We'll all try to be here next spring, and see all of our group return,
but now a "good day" and we're on our way. We're on the road again.

The Army Airport Sentry

The midnight hour is clear and so cold,
and I'm standing guard alone in "no man's land".
I remove my mind from the squeak of snow beneath my feet,
lest I freeze to death.
as I walk alone for two hours, alone and scared.

I try to think of something warm. It's hard to do,
but I must try and try again.
My mind drifts back to just this morning,
The barracks was warm and comfortable,
now my hands hurt, my feet and ears are cold.

The wind blows hard against my face and makes me turn away as I inhale.
The air cuts into my throat.
Ice forms about my mouth and nose as I breathe.
I wonder why there are no lights anywhere that I can see.

What was that? A noise inside the hangar over there!
There's no one here, is there?
What do I do? I un-sling my rifle from my shoulder
and into my gloved hands,
Trying to get my finger on the trigger. I can't!

I remove my glove and drop it to the tarmac
and have no time to pick it up.
I move along the building to a chimney and wait.
Still! Quiet! I have to breathe.
Perhaps it was nothing. I'm shaking. I'm sure, it was the wind!

I find a door and slowly open it. I step inside, my weapon ready to fire.
Suddenly a noise, I turn to fire at the movement, I am so scared!
A piece of metal has fallen. There's a broken window.

Back to my post, I look and find my glove is still there, and I put it on.
I re-sling my rifle and walk fast, moving to keep my feet from freezing.
I check my watch, trying to make the time pass quickly.

Mom and Dad have gone to bed by this hour.
It's past midnight. They are asleep.
I wonder who would try to steal an Army airplane, anyway?
It must be a threat or I wouldn't be here.

My sweetheart must be warm and comfortable.
I wonder what she is doing. Sitting by the fire,
reading or watching a movie on television with her parents?
I am getting sleepy. If I fall asleep I'll die.

I get colder just thinking about a fire, but I can't help what my mind thinks.
I wish I were drinking hot coffee in that airplane passing high in the sky.
They don't know I am here. I am so cold!

My shift will be over soon.
Checking the time will only make it seem longer.
There are no lights anywhere;
just the stars and the moon, making it seem even colder.
I'll go to see Marie this weekend and I'll be warm.
I can see a light in the distance then I hear the hum of a jeep. My relief?
The vehicle stops near the hangar, I yell, "Halt! Who goes there?"
"Sergeant of the Guard!" is the reply. "Report!"

"There is nothing to report Sir, Everything is normal!" I lied.
"Then change the guard!" he replied.
I wonder if I should tell him I was scared.
"No special orders, Sir!" I need to act brave.

The jeep was as cold as the airport, and bumpy,
but it was taking me to the guard shack.
"You O.K., soldier?" The Sergeant asked.
"Sir, Yes Sir, No problems, Sir, just a bit cold!"
I have four hours to sleep and warm my body; then it's my turn again.

Kindling

On a cold and snowy winter's day, in my last dreams of the night,
I begin to see the daybreak's glow, reflected on my windowpane.
Through my droopy, sleep-scarred eyelids, I see the colors of the sky.
They have made themselves known through the clear cold prisms
furnished by Father Ice.

The floor is cold and my steps make it squeak, objecting to my weight
as I hurriedly gather a little wood and a match to light the stove.
I place small slivers of the wood along the bottom of the iron grate
and hold the match to it, 'till it's aflame
and snaps back at the cold.

Placing the firewood on the flames, I feel the heat begin.
Escaping smoke stings my nostrils and I turn my head,
exhaling breath to expel the smoke. I search for cleaner air,
then continue fueling the flames.
I leave the fire door ajar.

I hear the whistling of wind as it blows through the window sash
and it sends the chill of the northlands flowing through the room.
I wrap the blanket around myself and hurry for my shoes
and place the coffee pot on the stove's flat top,
my hands held above the flames.

I watch as the flames spread along the length
and breadth of the kindling wood
leaving a trace of white, and blue, and red along the way.
It consumes itself, engulfing the wood that I had placed on top,
making hissing noises as it threads its way upward
to its destination of the uppermost log.

My body front is soon as hot as I can comfortably stand
while my back is cold in sharp contrast, and as I turn around,
I nervously back up, to get closer to the rapidly warming flames.
Now, I'm warm and comfortable as I hear the cry
of the winds that winter brings.

I watch the curls of smoke in white and gray and black arise
as if being called by their master hiding in the flue.
Now making a soft, low roaring noise powered by the windy draft,
a sound to match the flame's heat
brings, to my face, a smile.

The Wolf

On a dark and stormy night in the forest, a lonely animal cries.
Its sound is barely heard above the wind and driving rain.
But heard it is, its call is known, the giant timber wolf
has braved the storm to find himself a suitable den.

He is no stranger to these woods, all know of his desires
to find a home in which to mate and rear his brood.
and now, through his frequent visits, he has made his natural choice
of a place to locate his pack or family, a place of plentiful food.

His call is coarse, his voice is deep, his song a chilling chorus,
a wailing warning to all that can hear, from the unelected king.
And now, the woodland for miles around, once so peaceful and free,
yes, the area once so peaceful, is now claimed as the wolf's domain.

Even through the noise of the thunderstorm, you could hear the quiet fall;
a requiem for a way of life that has suddenly been taken away.
All other animals in these woods would have their lifestyles changed
in a cruel way undreamed of yesterday, certainly not desired today.

Even before the raindrops stopped, meeting places were being discussed.
a plan to retake the forest for the residents must be drawn.
Speeches were made, ideas were formed, discarded, and submitted again,
even though in anguish and desperation, the talks must continue on.

How can we defend our homeland? How can we fend our way?
How can we fight the mighty wolf that is so great and strong?
His tactics are brilliant; he works in teams, and we cannot find a way
to stop, or even stall him, in his conquest of our land.

"Mister Chairman, may I have the floor? May I offer my idea?"
Mr. Weasel spoke with the voice of a lion and the eloquence of a lord.
"I seem to remember my grandfather's tale, told around the winter's fires,
of a similar problem and his successful quest,
I can present it here tomorrow!"

So nothing was solved, nothing was sure
and all scuffled home with heads low.
Though Weasel promised his grandfathers tales,
not one plan was "in the mold".
They had found no ideas, the future looked dim, and quiet filled the air.
Maybe Weasel wouldn't show up again, after all he was getting quite old.

No adult could sleep on that moonlit night;
the stars made the country glow.
Fox looked through his window at the hills, wondering what was ahead.
"What on earth can we do?" he asked of himself,
"The wolves are certain to stay."
"They will find and devour us, one by one, unless we attack them, instead!"

Mister Skunk was pacing and thinking, with his hands behind his back.
He had tried to sleep in his bed of leaves, after taking a soothing bath.
"I have no way of fighting someone as large as a timber wolf!
but I have had some fun, making Ole Rabbit run,
when meeting him on the path".

Now, I haven't mentioned Old Bowser, the farmer's old hunting dog.
His bellows and barks disturb the animals, but he had never hurt any one.
His night was stripped of all sleep and rest
because he also had heard the wolf.
Aad he figured that he that would have to face it alone,
before this week was done.

When Tuesday arrived, the hall was packed, with the elders of the woods,
Buck Deer, from the dell in the foothills,
and Woodchuck, from the rocky ledge.
The squirrels and 'possums had taken their seats
to hear what Weasel had to say.
Skunk sat in his personal cubicle, for which every family had pledged.

The spectacled Chairman sat in his chair, waiting for the time to start.
The birds and chipmunks chirped away
as they sat with Rooster and the hens.
Mr. Fox and Rabbit, Squirrel and Possum stood up
while Duck made his way
to his seat in the middle, then Rat called out, "The meeting shall begin."

"Order! Order", called Chairman Coon, as he read the words from a book,
but that's the only thing he needed to say, so he gave the usual "Ahem!"

"We'll skip the normal procedures and get to the problem at hand.
the wolves are coming to our fair woods
and we certainly need to stop them.

"If I could, I'd like to say a few words" said Fox, from high in the stands.
"I would like to see the wolf sent away, but he must be given a chance."
This brought many "boos" from the audience,
and someone shouted, "Fox, sit down",
but Coon soon re-established order, by simply casting a serious glance.

Coon then stated the business at hand. "The wolf will have to go!
They are not like us; they are not good neighbors,
so we need to have a plan.
At our last meeting, Mister Weasel said that his grandfather had told a tale
of a successful action through cooperation, working together, to a man."

"Let's hear it then", Buck Deer snorted, "Let him tell us how!"
"Without further adieu", Coon said, stepping down,
"I present, Mr. Weasel to you!"
"Ahem! Good evening!" Weasel began, I live at the old Samuels place."
"Who cares? Answered one of the voices, "Just tell us what we can do!"

The meeting lasted until the sun came up. But no one batted an eye.
They were seriously contemplating taking a life,
which none had ever done before.
The story was told, a plan was made, a plan involving them all.
Some would make maps,
some would train others and some attend to the stores.

Then, on Wednesday night, at the meetinghouse,
the final plan was discussed.
Each would be checked for his duties and their equipment checked again.
There was plenty to discuss, during this meeting,
each man was asked to state
his position and suggestions in this, their last chance to sharpen the plan.

Mr. Owl had wisely selected the date;
it was perfect, the night of Hallowe'en.
Costumes to be worn had been stored in the barn,
and now were donned in a stall.
Mr. Goose was a cat, Groundhog was a bat and Fox was a big kangaroo.
Old Bowser, the dog wore an ostrich costume
and the raccoons wore nothing at all.

It was a lucky night and the moon was so bright
that the wolf would be hunting alone.
The pack had not arrived but for him to survive,
he would need to bring something home.
Now all started their journey to find their enemy,
and Weasel was leading the way.
The raccoons left early to wait at the lake, near some giant granite stones.

As they walked through the forest, all eyes were open,
and no one uttered a word.
Their army made for peculiar company, with an ostrich, bat and kangaroo.
They heard the wolf howl, very close and loud,
and Duck's beak started to clack,
but they all kept going, knowing the situation
and knowing what they each had to do.

The wolf was so close they could hear leaves rustle
as he walked directly toward them.
Then suddenly, he jumped into the pathway,
and growled, "What are you here to do?"
Bowser answered, in his best ostrich voice,
that they were looking for the zoo.
The wolf looked them over and bending his head,
asked, "What, in the world are you?"

"We come from Australia said "the kangaroo"
Fox, we taste awful, I've heard it said!"
But the wolf grabbed a monkey, saying,
"I'll try this one, I'll bite off the monkey's head".
Then out jumped Mr. Skunk and wet down
the wolf's trunk and all ran toward the lake.
The wolf passed them all, not bothering to catch them,
jumping into the water, instead.

Then as he swam, the wolf was pulled down, until bubbles began to appear.
Then his head would appear with a hand on his ear,
he would breathe and go down again.
When he wiggled no more, raccoons pulled him
to shore and revived him properly.
Weasel told him that this forest was no place for him,
"We have voted a hunting ban!"

The wolf snarled and spat, and said.
"I'll eat all of you, just as soon as I am free!"
A raccoon at each paw, he was cuffed,
then de-clawed and his eye teeth were removed.
Now, he lives in the woods eating porridge
and mushrooms, while hiding his ugly face.
His pack doesn't know where he made his home
and he's now following local rules.

Now, all share the forest, with the other animals,
that wish to live there in peace.
There are times that an issue may appear or be needed,
requiring your thoughts or labor.
But problems can be solved, if you share the resolve
that we must live in harmony.
Remember the story of the wolf, my friend.
"It's nice to get along with your neighbors!"

Christmas Wish

*

I
and you
must believe,
lest there be no hope,
a better world 'twould be
if we could only end the pain
that's inflicted by the greed of man.
Amen!

Memories of an Earlier Christmas

There was a chill in the air and frost on the grass.
There was ice on the pond; I wore boots.
Mom's eyes gleamed as she tended the fire.
The cattle huddled close by the barn.

On my walk to school it started to snow.
Hot chocolate was served to all.
The girls decorated with red and green roping
While the boys fetched a Christmas tree.

My school class sang carols now every day,
and the excitement was shared by all.
Everyone walked with a spring in his step,
Christmas was coming soon.

The teacher sang hymns and we all joined in.
Stories of the Christchild's Birth were told
of wise men on camels from a faraway land.
Mystery filled the air.

Dad and Mom shopped and then hid the gifts.
When I questioned my Mom, she just smiled.
The boys put a tree up while the girls popped corn
and strung it around and around.

Garland was draped, the tree crowned with a star,
we sang carols as our stockings were hung.
We sat by the fire as the embers died down
while "The Night Before Christmas" was read.

All the boys were together in one small bed
trying desperately to stay awake.
I tried to breathe quietly but my heart thumped loudly.
I awoke and it suddenly was dawn!

There was candy made of chocolate and coconut.
On this day, I could have more than one.
Dad and Mom had made breakfast and re-built the fire,
and all our stockings had been filled.

Sometimes, there were two presents, perhaps a knife or a gun.
At breakfast I was too nervous to eat,
then, I was off for a walk to enjoy my gifts.
I don't remember it being cold!

Church, on Christmas, was for singing carols.
My pistol showed through my clothes
which smelled of sulfur from capgun shots.
Gifts went to names that had been drawn.

Little things mean so much in my later years,
my memories of those seasons warm my soul.
It still brings a smile to this old wrinkled face
s I wish A Merry Christmas to All!

My Heritage

I was unlearned at my mother's breast
and since that time have made my quest
to conquer life in record time,
and set my goal for a life sublime.

Treading in my father's footsteps,
lest I falter, as we traveled and talked.
If I stumbled he would be there
to take my hand with love and care.

As I grew stronger with life's encounters
its wonder, joys, and sometimes strife,
I learned independence, to live on my own more
I was watched over and never alone

The years passed quickly as my life progressed
with the natural character that had been instilled
by those great and dependable hands
responsibilities to fulfill

When I reached adulthood, I would serve my country
serving as a soldier, to defend my fellow man,
as my fathers and brothers had done before me,
from an enemy in a alien land

I would be the best soldier that I possibly could be
true to my oath, I would stand tall
to defend my country's citizens' freedoms
and, if needed, I would give all.

I became a leader of many soldiers
deployed to the battlefield and then,
the enemy was engaged and battles were fought.
there, I had lost many of my men

.

More enemy came, but we fought on and on.
I remembered the words to that beautiful song,
"Whose broad stripes and bright stars,"
had a different meaning in this time.

The gun bursts finally got lighter,
with more and more time in between.
Then, slower and slower battle shifted,
the enemy was gone and some of my friends.

I eventually came home to raise my family
attempting to continue my past again.
My parents had left us with their guidelines
To raise our children to the standards they sought.

I question if I can do as well as they did,
and mold my children's character, as when I was a kid,
or if they thought the same when they were my age.
Perhaps, that is what they left me, that's my heritage.

Hey, Pretty Baby

On a bright summer's day in the early morning,
the first thing this baby girl heard
was, "Welcome to our world, little girl
and "Hey pretty Baby, come to me."

"You'll be loved and cared for in your new home
and dressed in the finest of clothes!"
"You'll be loved every moment of your life.
Hey, pretty Baby, come to me."

As she grew, and she grew into a beautiful girl,
there was plenty of love to go around.
The love kept coming and she kept hearing,
"Hey, pretty Baby, Come to me!"
.
When in her teens and a striking lady,
the boys begged for her company.
She won the admiration of the handsomest men
who called, "Hey, Pretty Lady! Come to me!"

She married a Prince, who held the world's respect.
Each day he would return from his duties
and call for his lady as he walked through the doors
With, "Hey, Pretty Lady! Come to me!"

Once upon a time when the Prince was away,
the Princess heard a knock on the door.
and she found a coach, with a voice from inside
saying "Hey! Pretty Lady! Come to me."

The coach drove away with the Princess on board.
she was taken captive by a King.
She never returned to her Prince, though he called,
"Hey, Pretty Lady! Come to me."

She grew old and gray, her body stooped and frail
as she served this King as his slave.
She was always expected to heed his beck and call,
of "Hey, Pretty Baby! Come to me."

Then one bright Spring day, in the early morning,
a Prince on a large white stallion, did appear.
With a sword pointed directly at the Princess, he said,
"Hey, Pretty Baby! Come to me".

She was whisked off to Heaven on this beautiful steed
to live there in peace forevermore.
When the time will come for her Prince to join her,
She'll call, "Hey, Pretty Baby! Come to me."

Tithing

The old minister awoke early on this winter Sunday morning,
made his way down to the kitchen where he drew a drink of water.
Gazing out upon the mountain, he could look deep into the woods now,
with no leaves to block his view, as they do from Spring through Summer.

Something moving in the cedars caught his eye this frosty morning.
Looking closer, 'twas a buck deer strutting in all of nature's splendor.
Breathing fog out through his nostrils as he bellowed to his harem,
presenting a beautiful picture through the old man's kitchen window.

The preacher thought of the coming winter,
with no meat stored in his smokehouse.
He also thought about his sermon, promised today for his congregation.
Perhaps, if he acted quickly, he could return in time for the meeting,
achieving all on just one Sunday. He hurriedly began his preparations.

Up the mountainside he labored, his throat raw from heavy breathing,
Onward the preacher hurried to the spot where the buck was seen.
Pausing oft' to listen carefully for any bellowing from his prey,
the old man kept his hot pursuit, no time to rest in between.

Then, when rounding Upman's knoll,
the preacher caught a glimpse of him.
His attention held by other business, the buck was oblivious to any sound.
Carefully moving even closer, the preacher loaded his high-powered rifle.
A single shot rang out this Sunday and the big deer fell to the ground

He had pushed hard going up the mountain and now,
finally, the preacher rested.
Now that time was of the essence, he must dress his hunter's bounty.
Securing the carcass to a high limb, it would be safe 'til he returned there.
He would come back after church services
and then carry it down the mountain.

Satisfied with his success now, his food secured for the long, cold season,
The preacher started his trek down the mountain,

toward his home nestled in the glen.
He was thinking about his sermon that he had written this past Thursday,
About all of God's children preparing. (Winter's food could be worked in).

Deep in thought and humming a hymn now,
his happy thoughts were of his luck.
Then suddenly, without any warning, a giant bear stepped into his path.
The preacher stopped, stone still and waited;
the giant bear stood up and snarled.
They stood too close to move his rifle; there was no room for him to pass.

The bear stood up, his paws extended,
his claws outstretched like razor blades.
He turned his giant head sideways, his face wore a menacing frown.
The preacher pulled his rifle upward and toward the menacing bruin,
but the bear proved to be the quicker,
knocking the gun down to the ground.

He grabbed the preacher in a bear hug,
squeezed him tightly, then threw him down.
The bear was growling and raising his lips,
baring large teeth under his snout.
Now the preacher rolled under a tree root, staying closer to the ground.
The bear circled around the tree root to find a chance to pull him out,

The preacher thought about his congregation,
eager to hear his Sunday speech
All about Heaven, keeping the Sabbath Holy,
and preparing for winter's deadly snare.
The preacher prayed for God's forgiveness, for hunting on a Sunday morn,
Then he prayed that God would protect him, from being eaten by the bear.

The bear stood beneath the carcass, trying to reach it, but it was too high.
He glanced back at the old man praying, as if to say, "I could eat that."
Then an idea struck, the preacher reacted a
nd with great speed untied his kill,
And as the bear had venison for breakfast, the preacher ran away, very fast.

The preacher ran right to the church house,
his congregation awaited him there.
He said "My people! On yonder mountain, lies an example for tithing time.
I gladly shared all my winter's rations, even though it is now late fall,
I gave all my meat to a poor stranger who had needs much greater than mine"

I gave up my winter's preparedness.
My store of plenty, I freely gave to him.
True tithe was revealed to me on that mountain.
Sharing with others feels so sweet.
When neighbors treat others kindly, it's a wonderful feeling I can't explain.
I beseech you to join me in free-hearted tithing,
in sharing your ration of winter's meat.

Please leave it in the Church's storehouse, which I keep behind my home.
Share your blessings in true tithing, as it was revealed to me.
Cast your eyes upon that mountain,
where your pastor and the stranger met,
And share with me in Holy Silence, my moment of sincerity.

A Winter s Monday

The air, warm and inviting a month ago,
causes me to shiver, and is painful to breathe.
I make my way carefully along the icy flagstone at the bottom of the stairs.
The only time I fell as an adult, was when I slipped on this same sidewalk,
falling on the heel of my thumb and causing a pain that lasted a week.

The snow from Sunday's storm, since mixed with salted sand and black oil
has been pushed into an ugly and lumpy row
beneath the suburban mailboxes.
It looked so heavenly white when it first fell.

As I placed my hand on the post to steady myself, I touched the small bell
my sister sent to me, but it didn't ring.
We were to ring it together when she next came for a visit but,
alas, that day would never come.
Now, after three years, the clapper has begun to rust but I can't bring
myself to take it down.

I soon take my exit into the big city, glancing involuntarily in the direction
of a glaring horn, and find the blower looking away from me;
they always look away.
I stop, and though in a flash of anger, let him go ahead.
He now waves as if he knows me.

Locking my car remotely, I joined the throngs of assembly-line workers
entering the building with scarves over their cold mouths, with red noses,
and no hint of vanity, until we are inside.
Then a thousand mirrors appear to begin the attempt to eradicate the ugly
scars of a winter's commute.

Daedalus

On a stormy night, on an angry sea
with a dozen sails ablow,
a tall ship faced the uncertainty
of a battle with a pirate fleet.
Her crew was young but sea-warrior trained
with a capable skipper and mate.
Her equipment was new and her furnishings proper
for a ship of the Spanish queen.

She was seven rods long and two rods wide
and the sweet smell of oil filled her hull.
She was quick to answer her helmsman's commands
and as fast as any battleship at sea.
Her sailors were young and had been well trained
in a school held especially for this trip.
They spent time off listening to their seniors
relive their tales of the sea.

Her sheets were trimmed to a starb'd tack
on her course with lanterns lit.
Her sailors were resting, her cannon stored,
she was trimmed to sail alone.
With a sailor on watch, a helmsman and a swab,
"All's well!" was called, and then
her bow was eased ten degrees to port
in a move to counter the seas

The sea froth slithered across her deck
as the scuppers had their fill,
but soon was gone, and another wave
refilled them all again.
Away from port for a fortnight, then two,
a rhumbline course she held.
"Twas the shortest way to the Caribbean
to search for her elusive prey.

The captain was tall, of Portuguese strain,
devoted to his ship and his queen.
He had shed his regalia for a more common dress
for the task soon to be at hand.
His hair shone copper beneath his hat,
his eyes had a penetrating stare,
in the color of the sea, which was turning now,
from blue-black to a sparkling green.

He spoke in tones that matched the task.
from his officers, he commanded respect.
All hands were expected to do their duty,
all for the good of the ship.
It was early fall, east of St. Augustine
when a sailor from up above
called, "Three masts abaft the starb'd beam
on a course the same as ours."

"Aye!" says the captain, I 'ave her in sight,
Keep an eye!", then, "All hands prepare."
The deck became active in war preparation,
and the cannon were locked in their place.
The deck officer reported, "Ready for battle, Sir!"
"Aye!" was the captain's reply.
"We'll hold our course, and identify her,
perhaps 'fore the dark of night."

Then nightfall came and the wait began,
the warriors slept on deck,
but when dawn arrived, they were all awake,
all eager to learn their fate.
All eyes looked West as the daylight broke,
but none called the "Ship in view",
then looking aft, they spied her bow
bearing down at battle speed.

"Battle stations, load cannon, stand ready!"
then "battle sails and stow the deck."
Any item movable was tied to its position,
then a disciplined quietness prevailed.
The roar of the bow wave seemed to be louder
as the sailors awaited their commands.
The captain looked to the helmsman and shouted,

"Mr. Marshall, bring her about!"

"Aye, aye, Sir", he answered and spun the wheel wildly
and the ship rolled to port with great force,
and soon, they were facing another great tall ship,
closing distance while bow to bow.
The silence was deafening, as the ships grew closer
the officers discussed engagement plans,
as given by their skipper, standing straight before them,
then each officer went to his men.

They would stay their course, and fire a warning shot,
and give the pirate ship time to respond,
and to identify herself, friend or foe,
by flying her colors in full view.
"Fire!" was the command, and the bow cannon belched,
then a tall splash was seen in the sea,
but 'twas answered by return of a cannonball
falling close to the battleship.

As their positions became near, the captain gave the orders,
"Hard alee" and the big ship lunged
to starb'd, then to port, as he reversed those orders,
to place the two ships abeam.
"Fire portside", and the guns roared, pieces flew through the air
as ship parts fell to the sea.
"Hard a'port, then hard to starb'd" and the ship rocked again
and left her stern to the pirate-ship

"About easy, Mr. Marshall!" then came the command,
and the ship smoothly changed her course,
turning toward the enemy, coming back to speed
to attack the pirate again.
"Prepare the bow cannon" which got the reply
that the cannon were ready to fire.
"We damaged her severely, we will ask for her flag!"
as the battleship neared the pirate's stern

The guns were reloaded and when alongside,
were all fired again.
The pirate ship went down leaving only debris,
her flag perched atop her mast.
The battleship headed southeast toward the islands

and spent a full year at sea
searching for yet more pirate-ships,
and destroying another three.

She then returned home and remained in port,
Awaiting her next command,
But pirates were no more of a problem
And her orders never came.
She was towed to sea and set afire,
Her days of war at an end.
But her majesty was remembered by her crew.
The tall-ship DAEDALUS.

Our First Date

A warm spring breeze drifts through my open window
as I awake this morning,
caressing me, not cutting my skin, as on mornings a month ago.
The tree, a mile away atop that hill, is bent so far south that now,
it will grow that way.
The lukewarm winds cause me to smile, even while nothing is on my mind.
With thoughts, only of good and happy things and places that I have seen,
I think of you, and try to remember how you looked
on that first day as we said adieu.

I wonder if you remember the things that we said
to each other on that wonderful night.
I will walk along the shore today and listen to the surf and rocks fight their
everlasting war over who will get their way, and I'll hear your sweet voice
blending softly with the sounds, as the seagulls laugh
and fly away before I get to where they are.
I'll think of our first date when we each brought a friend
and drove to Salisbury Beach.
It was the first time I had ever seen the sea. I had met a lifelong friend.

You sat in the sand beside me while my friend
spread his handkerchief for his date.
I then awkwardly offered mine, but you refused with a smile,
because it was too late.
I held your hand and we each told our stories and our dreams.
We smelled the salt air as it grew dark and the night flew by for me.
Too soon, we were at your door and had to say goodnight.
You walked me to the station where
I took the 11:32 milk-train back to the Fort.

Ah, for those days again, to have the feelings young people have,
just once more.
The excitement of your warmth, then your soft and tender kiss that left me
thinking only of our next meeting. I could think of nothing but you as the
days and nights dragged on.
As our romance bloomed, the sea became a friend of ours.

We spent many hours wondering endlessly on its shores, holding hands and
walking barefoot in it's cool sand,
growing deeper in love with each succeeding wave.

As our children grew, they too became addicted to the sea and its glory.
From morn to dusk they ran and laughed and played in the sand.
We had to force them to make time to eat their meals.
Our family grew strong alongside the waters, year by year.
Now all my thoughts are concentrated on those golden days of our youth,
and of the ocean, the kids, and of you and me.

We sailed together, teaching them all about winds and waves and the sea.
They were at home with sails or oars as other children played with toys.
Their skills were tested in the dangerous currents of the Merrimack.
Their finesse was shown in how easy they picked up the mooring buoy.
Each child soon presented us with two grandchildren, girls and boys,
which expanded our love lives even more.

Our grandchildren learned to love the sea and to sail with us.
We traveled to distant towns where we spent the hot summer weekends.
We planned sail trips of great precision and speeds
'till we made split-second times.
We fought seas and fog and winds through rains and sunshine.
In all our trips together, I only remember smiles, never a frown.
as they learned to enjoy the so-called "bad" days with the good.

Too soon, college came and one by one our crew was broken up
as they attended school in different and distant towns.
Our sails became further in between after the kids were gone,
then week after week, we were forced to sail alone.
We missed them and our days together, oh, so much,
but adult duties called them; they were now going on their own.

Now my trips to the ocean are far between, the sailboat has been sold.
I still drive to the jetties a few times a year, mostly in wintertime.
The ocean still excites me, especially during winter-driven storms.
Her whitecaps fly across the jetty's rocks to the sounds of a runaway train.
The sea breeze hits my face and I smile,
as today I do, with the warm spring winds.
I miss my youth, my dreams and you. Oh, to live my life again.

First Day-Last Day

Oh, my sweet love, as I await my end,
I remember the day I first saw your face and I remember the last.
If I could have another day, I would dream of you, lest I waste it away.
I would see only you on that day we wed
with smiles of joy and love for me.

As a running brook, our young love flowed
as we raised our children and watched them go and fulfill their dreams,
or was it our dream, spread over the land,
in several families? It seemed so fast.
Then we were old and I lost you, and I would mourn for eternity.

Now, as I come to join you in your rest,
I can only hope we will meet again
where I can gaze forever upon your face.
We can hold hands for a million years in eternity
before our journey begins,
to stroll through heaven in joy and peace and be loving partners again.

Breakup

In the middle of a starlit evening, on our favorite ocean beach,
sudden and relentless staccatos of heartbeats banging
outward in my pressurized chest,
like so many jackhammers, tearing my flesh in a hot, unconfined, and con-
fusing implosion of mind and body that I cannot tolerate or control.
You don't love me any more?

Squirrels And Quasars & Stuff
Prose and Poetry

AUTHOR'S FOREWORD TO
A CHRONICLE OF TRUE SHORT STORIES

Dear Reader;
I am very fortunate that my life has spanned the period from the Great Depression of the early thirties, to the studies of quasars in a new millenium. I witnessed the changes from "Pioneer America" to the current exploration of the remnants of the Creation of the universe.

I have eaten squirrel dumplings from necessity, was taught how to catch fish with my bare hands, and can hold my own in a discussion of quantum physics. I am one of a group of blessed people who have flown a Piper Cub with its doors removed, on a warm summer day. I have been entranced with a panoramic view of God's Perfectly Created Earth as I pushed the speed of sound, for many thousands of hours, from the captain's seat of a sleek jet airliner, while turning and climbing through clouds. Most times those clouds were as white as the winter snows and nearly as high as the sky, and sometimes they were dark and dangerous, but they were always spectacular.

I had a Dad who helped build a "back-country" church/school and then taught in it, even though he only had a sixth grade formal education. I was allowed total freedom to do the things that I enjoyed. As a young man, I found adventure in the military, then fell in love and spent my adult life, with a perfect partner, Marie. I have spent countless hours on my beloved sailboat "Nickelodean", watching seabirds, whales, and dolphins playing around me while the wind whistled through the ship's rigging.

God has allowed me a taste of Heaven through the stairways that others have laid before me. I give thanks to Him, my pioneering parents and loving siblings, who opened the door to the world and led, (and sometimes, pushed), me in.

I now present my story for your enjoyment. It is not a story about my life, but of how other people affected my life. Now, you are one of them. Enjoy!

"May God grant to my descendants the joy of life on earth that He has granted to me." AMEN!

Book Bonus #1

A Chronicle of True Short Stories

CONTENTS

The Beginning

When I grew up on the farm, we lived on top of a hill in a tiny house, with a small porch, that consisted only of a floor. A cistern stood at the end of the porch. A cistern does not provide water, it only stores it. This water had fallen as rain onto the rusted tin roof and traveled through rusted tin gutters and rusted tin downpipe into the rock-lined cistern for storage. We thought nothing about pushing aside "wiggle worms" (later found to be mosquito larvae) to get a dipper of drinking water. Maybe we would have noticed more if there had been something we could have done about it!

There was a lone, coveted patch of Bermuda grass that grew alongside this porch. It probably grew from the precious little wastewater my mother threw off that porch and into the yard. No matter, the patch was adopted for wrestling. We all had a great respect for that patch of grass and didn't walk or play there except when engaged in the serious sport of wrestling. I was pretty good, but no match for my seniors. The real wrestling took place between the older (and bigger) brothers. I also got educated there sometimes.

Once, my two oldest brothers, "Dall", (for Dallas), and "Boss"(for Marshall), were bathing in a washtub on the porch, while brother L.C. (Louis Carroll) and I wrestled. They were taking Dad's model "A" Ford to town. While they were tub-captive, my mother was explaining to them in no uncertain terms, that she had discovered they had been hanging around with some "bad" girls. Even today I remember their names! I only hope those ladies straightened up 'cause my mother was onto them!

L.C. is the brother that is my next sibling upward, being four years my senior. Sometimes, such as now, that age difference doesn't matter. But when I was eight, I stood in awe of the powers of this twelve year old giant! I spent thousands of my non-school hours with him talking, singing and doing chores. One of these chores was sawing wood. My father would cut a tree down and leave L.C. and me to saw it into stove-wood lengths and split it for my mother's fuel. Power saws were well into the future! We used a crosscut saw, with L.C. and me stationed at either end; we sang many a duet while the saw chewed its way through the tree.

I can blame L.C. for leading me into a lot of situations! A friend and we had a secret place in the woods, complete with sandpit and skillet where we enjoyed parched corn and frog legs. We even found a farmer's watermelon patch for an occasional dessert. But one day, while relieving a farmer of a particularly beautiful melon, we heard, "Huh-O, I've got you now!" I still can hear that dreaded voice, precisely as it sounded then! We ran as fast and as far as we could, but he had already recognized us. We were constantly in trouble. Once when racing a buggy as the Romans did, Jimmy Thompson, a neighbor, fell out and the wheel of the buggy ran over him. He wasn't hurt physically, but I can't say his pride was boosted. On another occasion, I was riding a horse alongside a tobacco drying barn and startled a big sow that had been sunning herself. She jumped up, making a loud grunting noise. This scared the horse and she ran down the gravel road, losing her footing in the crushed rock surface, and fell into a ditch. Luckily, I fell first, and into the lowest and smallest part of the ditch. The horse, knowing I was there, held herself off of me while I crawled out unharmed. Noticing the size difference, I appreciated that. But I'll have to admit in all fairness, that L.C. didn't have anything to do with that event.

We had many good times and some funny times together. L.C. decided we could make some money by trapping for fur. He set a trap near some rocks on a hill about a mile from our house. Next day, on the way to school, we checked the trap and found that our business was already successful. We had caught a skunk. We then attempted to mix business with education, by joining our classmates. As I remember it, the teacher wasn't thrilled, to say the least! I credit L.C. with much of my business education!

One day, while I was outside the schoolhouse, doing a chore for my first grade teacher, a car drove in the school driveway. The driver asked me to ask the teacher if he could show a movie in the one- room school that night. I asked, and she agreed to let him use the school. He then asked me to ask my mother if he could have supper with us as there were no restaurants in the area, and of course my mother agreed and, because of her hospitality, we all went to the movie free of charge. I had never seen a movie. I was excited!

Needless to say, when the movie started, I was in the front row, directly in front of the white screen. Even as the title appeared upon the screen, I was frightened, then greatly embarrassed, when the first lion I had ever seen attacked me, head-on. I fell over backwards into the next row. Everyone in the room laughed at me. However, I totally enjoyed "Clyde Beatty, the Lion Tamer".

"Let me look at your ears!" Mom was saying as we left home real early in the morning. Dad had been up before dawn to milk the cows and feed the animals, eat breakfast and prepare for the trip. Mom had a way of finding dirt in my ears even when I was clean. I may have had some skin disease that looked like dirt. She would wet the end of her handkerchief and poke her finger around my ear with great force. I always yelled in my survival efforts, but to no avail.

"What's a funeral, Dad?" I asked. I stood right behind sister Wanda, who was always there in the front seat between Dad and Mom. I favored the right shoulder of my dad because I could imagine that I was driving and, at the same time, I could stay away from Mom's inspections and repairs. "It's when people get together to remember and pray for the soul of a person who died!"

Grandma Green had died. My parents had expected it. They had ordered my first suit of clothes from the Sears, Roebuck catalogue and it had been delivered to our mailbox. I had seen pictures of the suit and, when it arrived, of course I wanted to wear it. However, I was only allowed to try it on and it fit fine. It was light green with short pants and a white shirt. I also had new shoes and I looked great.

Dad did real well in driving the old A-model Ford. He was smooth and I could anticipate what he was going to do even before he did it. We soon arrived at Grandma's house where there was much activity. My cousins from Knoxville, Spartanburg and Miamisburg, Ohio were there. There were lots of people from around our area too. I kept busy getting acquainted again and showing off my new clothes, all the while hoping to keep from getting dirty. Soon a big long black car came and some men went into Grandma's house. I knew where her bedroom was because she had asked to see each of her grandchildren individually, a few nights before, and I had a conversation with her after all the others had gone in to see her. Now everyone became very quiet. I became quiet because my mom was crying and my dad gave me a "be quiet" look. Then the men carried a long silver box from the house and placed it in the big black car, Dad said, "Keed, Come on and get in the car." I still don't know what that name means but that's what I was called and Dad was always formal. It suited me fine that we were driving somewhere again, I just couldn't figure why everyone was leaving at the same time. As soon as we started I asked, "Dad, what was in that big silver box?"

All the cars drove in a line that must have been ten miles long. I had never seen this done before. At first, we passed some unfamiliar places but soon the scenery became familiar. We were going "across the mountain" where we went often, to where I was born. I didn't know the names of the mountains, except one named "Clinch". It didn't seem right, naming a mountain anyway. Mom cried most of the way and I watched Dad drive around the curves and shift gears up and down the hills. Mom always cried soft and quiet. I never could figure why a person would cry this way. When I cried, I always made all the noise I could. Most people did! You wouldn't know Mom was crying until you saw the ever- present "attack" handkerchief in her hand. She would cry sometimes when she was happy too. I could never figure her out. Sometimes when we were sitting together in our porch-swing, she would cry real quiet. During these times, I kept my mouth shut and took over the pushing of the swing.

Soon, we arrived at Yellow Branch Church. I was born a few hundred feet from this church. By the time we parked and got out of the car, the men had already put the big box in the church. We went inside and someone was already playing the organ and everybody started to sing. Then the minister spoke for a while about Heaven and families and such. They had partly opened the box and people were crying. Then we all formed a line and walked by the open box and I could see Grandma's face and a little of the rest of her, all dressed up and she had her hands crossed as she sometimes did when she sat in her rocking chair. The minister, Johnny Coffee, read from the Bible and added some of his own words. He said that Grandma was married in Yellow Branch Church and that she was a good person and had gone to live with God, which threw me a curve because I could still see her. I immediately tried to get a clarification of this phenomenon from Dad but he gave me that "be quiet" look and I always obeyed it.

Everybody sang "We'll understand it all bye and bye", a couple of other songs and then "Nearer, My God, to Thee." Then some of us walked by and looked again and I'm sure others saw what I saw. We then drove, still in a line to a hill where, I am sure I had been. I don't know why but that whole place was familiar. My cousin Billy Ray found me and said "Come on, I have something to show you!" We crossed the road in front of the big car and went into the woods. Climbing down a steep slope, we came upon two caves. A river ran out of one cave and then directly into the other. We explored this find but, to keep our families from leaving without us, we soon climbed back up the hill and joined them. The people were now saying their good-byes. The box had been buried in the field and covered with flowers. Soon, we were in Dad's car, going home without the other cars. "Dad?" "Yes, Keed!" still being formal, "Where's Grandma?"

After my older brothers left for the war, in 1942, the farm was quiet. I used to lie on the grass wrestling mat and watch the airplanes fly over on their way to war, and I would wonder where my brothers were. I used to think that a battlefield was much the same as a pasture with a fence. Dad listened to the news a lot when the battery in his radio was good enough. We didn't have electricity and frequently, no good batteries either.

Before he left for the war, older brother Dall had acquired a collie pup named Ben. Ben and I were together all the time. We moved to a different house during the war. Dad had gone to work in a defense plant. One day, immediately after the end of the war, Ben disappeared. I didn't learn, until I was 67 years old, that someone I knew had killed him. It has been good for all of us that I didn't know. However, it had happened before. Remember the porch on the farmhouse? We had a pit-bull that had been given to L.C. by Grandpa Green thirteen years before. "Fritz" came home torn up badly. He crawled under the porch to die. I was told that perhaps a bear had tangled with him, and I accepted that. I had to crawl under the porch to retrieve the body for burial. Now, also at 67 years, I find that an acquaintance had shot him too. Neither of the dogs chased livestock or stole eggs, habits unforgivable on a farm. God, forgive my hatred for the memory of those two people. In all the intellectual and spiritual strength that I can muster, I believe those people are the lowest creatures that God ever created. I hope God agrees with me!

We all had to help with the chores on the farm. There were chores, other than wood sawing, to which I lent my superior skills. I also chopped "Johnson" grass out of zillions of mile-long rows of corn, in the hot Tennessee sun. I also milked cows before and after school.

As farm boys, we did live on the edge. We would swim in swamps where cottonmouth water-moccasins were basking on shore. We lifted rocks so that "Ben" could grab a snake and shake it to death. We even ran through pens where sows were protecting their new-born piglets. The sows would try to catch us. If we had fallen, we would have been promptly dissected.

Yea! I remember a lot of wonderful childhood things and family happenings. I remember the cars that my Dad had when I was a kid. The very first vehicle that I remember was the "A" model Ford, a four-door sedan where I could stand in the back, directly behind Wanda, and between and behind Dad and Mom, and look across the long hood. The windshield was vertical and could be opened when the weather was hot. I now shudder to think that the gasoline tank was at the base of the windshield. A float, inside the cap, would push a wire up above it, so that the driver could see how much gasoline was available. Even refueling was an adventure. We would go to the grocery store and stop beside the tall pump. Someone, usually L.C., would push and pull the long handle on the pump until the desired of gasoline was pumped up into the glass barrel, which had a brass bell at each gallon mark. When the gasoline reached each bell, it would ring. He would pump the amount needed, pay the store clerk, and then squeeze the handle to allow the gasoline to flow into the tank.

The "A" model also had a radiator with the fill cap located directly in front of the hood. All cars were like that, but our car had a working chrome propeller built into the cap, which gave me great joy to watch as we moved along. With my sister in the front seat between Mom and Dad the six other children were crammed in the back. I stood up, which gave me more room. Now I understand why children got married and left home! It sure was hot in the back seat on a Tennessee summer day and one of us, I won't say which, would sometimes get motion sickness.

I started my education in a one-room school named Shady Grove. I was treated to Christmas plays, ice cream suppers, cakewalks, Saturday shopping trips to town, molasses stirs and taffy pulls. Hayrides were part of my farm entertainment. I was raised on a farm that covered miles, giving me the freedom to vocalize and exercise to my heart's content. No one ever stopped me from singing and yelling at the top of my voice, and the scenery was among the most picturesque in the world. I enjoyed every minute, from catfishing to watching ever-present cumulus clouds being used as a playground by turkey vultures, to a nap under the maidenhair fern that sat on our front porch. Here in my paradise, I delighted in trips to the mill with Dad, and Sunday visits with friends. The world was so easy to enjoy! Jonquils were called Easter flowers and summers went on forever! Everyone loved and cared for me and I shall cherish each one of them forever.

I remember the exact minute of my first sighting of an airplane. My cousin explained this flying machine to me, and remarked that it was carrying people. I announced then and there that someday, I wanted to pilot of one of those airplanes and thirty years later, I realized my dream. During the war years, I was delighted to watch hundreds of planes fly over in formation, being delivered, I found later, from a factory in Willow Run, Michigan to Pensacola, Florida for shipment.

Two of my brothers were drafted into the Army early in World War Two. I thought that, with such a low number, many more wars were planned and that was rather exciting! My father took a job in a defense plant that made bomb plugs. My two older sisters married two of the most wonderful people, whom I would dearly love for all of my life! I was left with one brother and one sister at home. My father moved our family to a different house, within a mile of railroad tracks, where I spent many hours and days observing troop trains. It was my patriotic duty to wave to each and every soldier as he passed on his way to war. I also became an "expert" in the equipment being delivered. I was one of the few who thoroughly enjoyed WWII.

In my youth, I was surrounded by and tutored in music, math and science, yet I was unaware of the fact that I was being taught. My precious father presented education as fun and made the most difficult of lessons an enjoyable game. For example, he teased me with this trick. Pick any number, multiply it by two, add ten, divide by two, and now subtract the original number you selected; your final answer will be five; half of whatever was added. It was a long time before I figured out how this worked, and when I did and told my father, he just laughed softly. He had taught me what double-talk math sounds like.

I also entered another segment of my education here! Across the road, through the pasture, across the creek, over the hill and in the woods, there was an old Civil War gun emplacement. Many of these "bowl" shaped areas are still around today grown over with trees. This area had once been a section of North Carolina and it was one of the many places where you could find both Confederate and Yankee sympathizers or traitors, according to your preferences. Here, I could find "hobos" at almost any time of day or night with their campfires, stories and music. They told of big cities and brushes with the law and railroad police that they called "dicks". They played banjos, guitars, French harps and Jews harps. They reminisced about their families and jobs they had held. The smartest part of my brain told me to be scared, but the adventurous part proved dominant. I returned there many times. I must admit that, other than asking my mother for food, which she always provided, they were perfect neighbors.

We moved to the city when I was twelve and entering the seventh grade. I hated it! I walked ten miles every day to catch a bus that drove me another ten miles over rough roads to the school I had left. No one ever mentioned it to me but I suppose my teachers knew or they wouldn't have let me ride the bus. Eventually, I had to start the eighth grade in the city school. My surroundings were different but enjoyable. I made friends quickly and was delighted to have such a selection at hand. I had never had so many people around me. New adventures of hiking, football, roller-skating, golf caddying, trading labor for tickets to the carnivals and circuses and pool presented themselves. Yes, pool! Just like in "River City", pool contributed to my delinquency at school! I was smart in school, but hated being locked up. I missed my freedom, my animals and my nature greatly! Even though I began to like my city life, I wanted those hills and mountains and their surrounding glory more every day but my return was not to be. It would be 50 years before I would return to my beloved land, the farm.

In 1936, there appeared a beautiful baby sister named Wanda Mae. While I remember very little about "Wan" being an infant, she and I became fast friends and playmates. My closest brother L.C. would sometimes be with my older siblings or away at school, so I was "stuck" with my sister, but sometimes I could work her into one of my adventures.

Wan was always a good sport and would forget what trouble we had found last time we played, so I would never say she was stupid, just forgetful! We roamed all over the hills of the farms and looking back, I don't know how those little legs could walk that far. She would get testy once in a while but only once did I hit her. It didn't hurt her and she didn't notice that I had hit her, but I found that it did hurt me because I loved her so much and I am, (and she has always loved this part), eternally regretful.

I was into aircraft engineering and used Wan for the position of test pilot. But that "Flight" usually didn't last long enough to think about retirement, although maybe she did wonder about health insurance. I made beautiful, safe aircraft from coat hangers and flour sacks, soaked in a mixture of flour and water which, when dried, held together nicely. I also conducted stage shows of gigantic proportions, and who else could be the star? Even when we grew up, I'm not sure she appreciated fully the start that I gave her in the entertainment world, simply due to this exposure.

Once, I decided to stage a "Minstrel" show. I handled all the promotion and direction, the important stuff. She knew more music than I did, so I knew she was right for the part. I found tar along the crossties of my beloved and nearby railroad tracks and, after a little cooking and cooling, I lavishly applied her makeup. Well, you would have thought that my mother had never been educated in the world of show business either! My beautiful star had her makeup removed with kerosene, and her long blonde hair washed a thousand times to remove the sweet smell of that kerosene. Show business and aircraft engineering were just two of the fields of my endeavors that were permanently placed off limits by Mom.

I mentioned earlier that I took my Mom, indeed my family, for granted. I certainly did, and I believe that if a child is secure, he should. I know that I don't want my children to thank me for their life. But I do believe that, when you leave that secure home environment, you should realize that that luxury is over. That is how it was with my parents and all my siblings. When I left for military duty I probably didn't even say goodbye. I was just going somewhere to do something else. But after a few days, I found myself without my mother, my father or my siblings. I had lost that innocent feeling of security in which I had grown up. I missed my family terribly as I slowly adjusted to army life but, at the same time, I learned to not take them for granted.

There is a profound part of military life, in which I was trained to help new recruits overcome. First, the men are stripped of their independence by all the yelling and confusion. But it is a tried and true, highly organized, chaos. This operation goes on for a few days, and then each one finds his consolation and independence within the cooperation of the unit. You can see the change, as each man becomes a part of his unit. With no first name recognition, he is allowed no individualism and melds into a new position within his new world. Then, each is recognized with an assignment that only he will be expected to fulfill, and will be depended upon, by his leaders and his fellow soldiers, to be responsible for his job within the team. His pride returns.

I now know what work each member of my family did in the building and support of our family unit. I now know how we unwittingly worked together, and not only poked fun at one another, but hugged one another with arms and words. When I return home in my old age, I am met with deep love and respect from all my siblings. Well, all except two. I lost my oldest sister Mildred, "Bill", recently to Alzheimer's and my lovely buddy "Wan" died of cancer in 2003. I don't think any of us take the other for granted any more. Wanda and I spoke weekly on the phone and I could always depend on her to fill my mind with cheer. I will forever miss her laughter.

Before leaving the "family history" section of my story, I must tell you that there has been more than a little unrest within my ancestry. Two of my great uncles robbed a bank in North Carolina, had a shootout with the Sheriff in Tennessee, and were apprehended, tried, and electrocuted.

And before that event, the Greenes and a neighbor, the Jones', had a feud that caused havoc in the Cumberlands, and was quelled only by stationing a Tennessee National Guard Unit in Rogersville just to quiet things down. It evidently did so, but not before being classified as a feud, second only to the Hatfields and McCoys, and a few people from both families were killed.

It seems that a pig strayed through a hole in the fence, and into the menu of the neighbor, starting a long-running argument between the families. The U.S. Civil War had started, and one of the neighbors came home from his assignment only to get shot by the feudal opposition and somehow, a baby was killed. Many of the citizens in that area were sympathizers with the Rebels and many were supporters of the Yankees. There were families that had soldiers in each of the armies. That fact must have caused a lot of conflict and heartbreak. I am glad that I was not there.

When older and we recall our life's events, some mean more to our soul, than others do. That first school, Shady Grove, was my foundation and pillar. I took my children a thousand miles to stand in its doorway, and to see what I saw that made it one of the most treasured things in my life. But I realized then that it was my treasure, and my children could not view it with the same eyes, heart and love that was instilled in me by my precious parents. Even though my children could only listen with their ears, I hope they can relay the stories of the calmer and more reverent life in which I was raised, to my great grandchildren. I apologize that I could not give the same type of life to them.

One summer I was blessed with the chance to take my oldest grandchild back to that farm. She quietly surveyed the rolling hills, the green grass with cattle grazing, surrounded on two sides by mountains, and for a long while she drank in the solitude it provided with a smile on her face, and then she asked me how I could leave it. She made my day! But I know she can't hear my mother's sweet voice calling to the peacocks she used to feed, or the "pop-pop-pop" of the John Deere tractor; nor could she feel the warm joy that I felt while walking home from school on a summer's day, as I did then. Ah, the sweet, sweet sounds of the love and security of youth. Sweet, sweet sounds that became sap for my soul; sounds that I would treasure all my life. Those sounds are now gone forever, except in my memories. "Listen with your heart, sweetheart, your ears can never hear it." As we walked around the quiet old farmhouse, I remembered a song that my family would often sing, that fit so well that day;

> "I called and I called but nobody answered.
> I looked everywhere but no one could I see.
> Then, I knocked on the door, as I oft' had before
> but nobody answered me."
> I surely miss those days.

The Fishing Spot

One hot day, when I was about ten, I guess, I decided that I might as well go fishing. We had a pond on the farm that was divided by fences. About six different pasture fields had access to the pond that way but the fence went right out through it so the cows or horses couldn't go to the other's field. I don't know why. I never heard of any bickering over who had the best grass. They just took what you gave them and walked away.

Anyway, I dug some worms from about the only place I knew that you could find worms. Mom had a garden and she kept it pretty well plowed to where it was easy to dig. Oh, she got pretty mad once in a while at me for "ruining her garden" but I figured that she was mad at someone else and needed me to be the sounding board, which was all right. She was a good person.

I dug some and noticed that the worms that I found were really puny, but they go deep in hot weather just when you need them, and to forgo my having to work harder for the fat ones, I would just use these. So, I got a pole and a stopper and some string and a cob for a float, tied them all together and went on down to the lower edge of the pond. It was the low part of the land, so a stone dam had been built at one time and the road curved alongside it, making it easy to walk to. You shouldn't work up a sweat to go fishing. My brother told me that fish can hear you talking and so I figured they might be able to smell a sweaty person and move to the other side of the pond.

My favorite spot was on top of this rock dam a few feet from a small weeping willow tree. I say a few feet; maybe it was more sometimes because a big cottonmouth water moccasin slept under that tree on a rock most of the time I had been fishing there. He was sure there today, sound asleep. He doesn't bother me and I sure won't wake him up either.

I had the place all to myself, well, the snake and myself, but we were fine with the arrangement and I had already set my line and was busy thinking about things. Fishing is a good thing to do when you want to think about things. At least I had plenty of time between bites, to think. I didn't have much to think on sometimes but I tried.

I had been just watching my corn cob float and turned to look behind me for some reason, and saw her coming. I was shocked! It was the old lady from over the hill. She lived the opposite way to the one she was coming from. She was real skinny and wore a bonnet and long dress and she walked like she had two weeks to get wherever she was going. She was walking real slow straight up the lane that comes from our main barns. Now, my mother always told me not to bother people. She told me to be especially careful to not bother old people and especially careful about old ladies. Especially, if I didn't know them too well. I didn't know any too well. Old people were usually real quiet and secretive. Except my Aun't Carrie, my dad's sister, who visited sometimes from Ohio. She laughed and joked and acted just like she wasn't old. But this old woman, the one that's coming up the lane, lived over the mountain that we were facing, up past the row of walnut trees. My brother called them "warnet trees", I don't know why, but he did. Maybe he didn't want to bother his tongue to move to say walnut. Some people say "irund" when they mean island. I guess that's no worse than putting the "s" in island in the first place. Who does those things? Maybe there is a boss teacher someplace that tells other teachers how to spell things. For sure, I bet she doesn't live on an irund. I guess I'm for anything that saves time and effort, especially in the summer. My brother and I sometimes talk without mooing our ips, an we say ords ike irund and warnets, so ue on't ave to oove our ongue. Something just pulled my float a little bit.

I have to walk through a field beside the old woman's house when Mom sends me to the store. When you get to the end of the walnut trees, you have reached the top of the mountain and you have to go to your left because a meteor had hit there, many years before, they say. There was a deep hole, shaped like a cone, as deep as the trees were high. At the bottom of the cone was a pond, with, "God only knows" swimming in it and a cave facing the pond, with the same things living in it. When Grandma Green died, I found a cave, just like it. Except it had two big caves and a creek ran out of one and into the other. I didn't find it, my cousin Billy Ray did, but while people were at the cemetery, he took me down there. There was a small coyote inside that barked at us like a dog until we left.

Anyway, she would have to go around the meteor cone and down the other side to her house. I just never saw her walk to or from. She always just appeared like a ghost. That's what was scary. I had seen her standing on the bank of the pond, over by the second pasture before, fishing. She stood real still. I just can't stand still like that for very long. Those thoughts made me a little nervous. I was in sight of my house, so I could yell and Mom would hear me. I learned to yell real shrill-like, just like a whistle because I couldn't whistle as loud as my brothers could. But Mom sang when she was alone. She sang kind of "opera" stuff, and loud. So if she was feeling like singing, I could be in a lot of trouble.

I looked straight at my cob float and she walked right up close to me, scaring me half to death. She didn't speak and as far as I could tell, she didn't even breathe. Of all the places on the pond, she walked right up close to me and didn't say a word. Perhaps, someone told her to never speak to ten-year-old kids, especially while they are fishing.

I tried to look straight ahead at my float and then "wall" my eyes, (that's when you turn your eyes as far as you can), without moving your head. I never heard of walling anything except your eyes. I tried to see her face, which I had never done. With that deep bonnet, no one could. What if she had a blank face?

I could see her shoes, just under her long dress. She wore shoes that real old women wear. You know, they look like Dad's work shoes except they are for old women. I haven't had shoes on my feet since March, nor sox, nor underwear, nor belt, nor shirt, nor anything else except my necklace. I removed the lead from a roofing nail and smashed it around a string. I wear it all the time to prevent nosebleeds in the hot sun. Dad says that it's not magic, it's that lead always stays cold and thickens the blood.

She opened a paper bag and took out a glass jar. Then she pulled out the biggest roll of worms I had ever seen. Those worms were wiggling like they were going to attack the fish. My worms would always give up, and lay down as soon as I found them. I was so interested in those worms that I almost forgot to look at her face. My walled eyes were getting tired. She took a worm and just stuck the hook through it, picked up her pole and swung it into the pond.

People just don't put worms on their hook that way. In the first place, the fish will see the hook. In the second place, the fish will pull the worm off and leave with it. Besides, there's a proper way of placing the worm on there. You pick up the worm and hold it with its end exposed. Now, Mom also told me to never get into discussions like this, so I'm going to tell you that you can start the hook into either end. I don't know which end is the mouth, if you are delicate. Just pretend that it is the mouth. The worm has a hole all the way through, so just thread him on, leaving the squirmy end free to squirm and attract the fish. Also, if the end squirms, you know you started the hook in the mouth and not the other end. I decided that I had to tell her or she would go home hungry and stay hungry.

While I was waiting to see her face before telling her that she was making a mistake, this fish, probably a sick or confused one, got stuck on her hook. She almost hit me with the thing. I dropped my pole and jumped away and she laughed a cackling laugh. She apologized and I saw that she wasn't so bad after all but I would still be careful.

She said, "Have you caught anything?" Of course, I said something to the effect that I always catch some catfish and sometimes carp, although I didn't especially like carp, because of the bones. Well, she started talking and I wondered if I should tell her about her worms and about the fact that she was fishing in a bad spot. No fisherman can tell you what a "good" spot is. You develop the "feel" for that over the years. I was in a good spot; she was in a bad spot. Where the cottonmouth was sleeping was a "good" spot but I wouldn't advise her to take it. I was feeling better about talking to her as long as Mom didn't look out and see me bothering her. Then, I would get scolded for it, I'm sure. So I told her where the better spots were. She said, "I'll rather stay here and talk to you, if you don't mind!" Of course, Mom always said, if the old people actually asked you to do something, you had to do it, so I let her stay. I couldn't catch anything because she started talking and talking and scaring the fish away from my spot and while they ran away, they got "snagged" on her hook. Soon, she had three or four of my fish and said goodbye.

As she walked up the wagon trail and under the walnut trees, I watched, waiting to see where she vaporized but she knew I was watching and delayed it until she was out of sight. You know, I don't remember ever seeing her again either. It gave me something to think about after I changed spots. That's another thing good fishermen know; good fishing spots can change without notice.

The Train Wreck

"C'mon!" L.C. said, as he started his journey. That's about all it took to get me trotting along with him. He could move quickly when properly motivated. I was ten years old and an acceptable companion to the 14 year old when no one else was available. "Where we goin' L?" I asked. "To Whitesburg!" "What for? We goin' to walk all the way to Whitesburg?" I asked. "Been a train wreck! You want to go?" He sometimes asked me things after we had begun walking so that I could stop walking and return home if I had a mind to. But I'm no fool. "There ain't no way I'd miss a train wreck." I loved the trains. There was always excitement along the tracks. Being the "Crossroads of Dixie", my hometown sat right in the middle of the nation's north-south and east-west crossroads for rail shipping and travel. A train passed on these tracks about every fifteen minutes, twenty-four hours a day. I had learned to love the steam engine's lonely whistle at night. It was like a trickle of a mountain stream to me, and remains so, even today.

L was a hundred feet ahead of me because I figured that, if I laid back a bit, he would slow down, but not today. He just kept going. Then, looking down, he stopped suddenly and I soon caught up. "Must have come from an ambulance!" he answered, without a question. He pointed to a ball of cotton on the side of the road. "What?" I asked. "Blood!" He walked again, with even more determination, towards Whitesburg. "Wow!" That made the gravity of our trip hit home. Blood? That much of a train wreck? Now I begin to walk as fast as I could and started asking him questions. "What happened? Why did they wreck?" "The train on the main line jumped the switch and hit the sidetracked train head-on!" "Anybody get hurt?" I asked. "Guess they're all dead!" he replied.

I was thinking, "I have thousands of questions but why do I have to ask? Why don't people just tell you all they know, and where did he get all his information, anyhow?" All my breath was being used to keep up and I couldn't ask any more. So we sped along in silence becoming aware of summer-hardened bare feet slapping the red-hot asphalt. We usually walked the tracks on our journeys, but I guess we were keeping to the highway 'till we could find some answers. Besides, an ambulance could pass along the road and we might miss it. We knew that ambulances were always Cadillacs and they really went fast.

We arrived at the site of the wreck to find that all that L had said was true. Giant cranes were bending down and people were screaming orders. We stayed a ways back, wiggling our way to increasingly better viewing spots. I had never seen this many people in Whitesburg. As a matter of fact, I had never seen this many people in one place in my life. Everybody had beaten us to the scene. The focus was the two enormous black engines lying on their sides, eerily silent. I had never seen a quiet steam engine. The crane had a mouth with teeth and it picked up large bites of loose wheat from a pile that was mixed with millions of lemons. The crane opened its mouth and almost humanely put the wheat and lemon mixture in another pile. Then, I saw the reason this mixture was handled so carefully. Parts of a person were removed from the mouth before the mixture was dropped. Only then did it dawn on me that there were real people in this strange mess.

Some months later, I accepted an invitation from a sidetracked crew to come aboard the engine of their locomotive. I looked out the windshield, which is on the side and saw a double red light on the signal. I knew that it meant that another train was coming from the opposite direction and would arrive shortly. It was still fresh on my mind that this was how the wreck happened in Whitesburg! I became a little nervous, then suddenly and without warning, the firemen stepped on a release that threw open the door to the firebox with a loud clang. I could have killed myself as I jumped from the ten-foot high cab to the ground, landing on the crushed rock. Then and there, I knew that I had completed my last free steam-engine tour. However, I still love those big black, noisy steam-engines. I didn't like the diesels and still don't, even if they are more efficient. Some things were so romantically beautiful that, sometimes, I wish they had never been changed.

In 1948, when I was sixteen years old, while mowing the lawn on a hot day, I stopped to enjoy a bottle of cold chocolate milk. Sitting on the grass and leaning against a rose trellis, I lifted the bottle to drink. Overhead, I noticed a round silver dish, slowly oscillating and traveling on a fast westward course, toward Knoxville. I ran to call my Mom, dropping the bottle and spilling the milk on the lawn. I pointed the object out to her and I suggested that perhaps I should call one of the newspapers for which I worked. Mom explained to me that people who saw such things were considered strange, so I took her advice and didn't report the sighting. Some time later I learned that, in all probability, this phenomenon was not a weather balloon, because it was traveling at a high rate of speed and on a westerly course. Weather balloons are slow and always follow the predominately easterly air currents. After an aeronautical career, I still have no explanation for this object, but I survived!

Pellissippi

My friends and I were in the Boy Scouts together and we spent many summer days hiking to the fishing house on Cherokee Lake that the Tennessee Valley Authority had left for that purpose. The house had doors, windows, and wood bunks on the walls. We spent many nights frying the fish we had caught, laughing and telling tall tales. One year we went to Boy Scout Camp. I did not have the necessary thirteen dollars to finance this trip, so my scoutmaster allowed me to clean his cellar where his dog had spent his winter days unrestrained, if you know what I mean. Then, as if that were not enough, I had to paint a picket fence that separated the scoutmaster's yard from one owned by an enormous bulldog that, through it's eyes and nasal sounds, swore it would kill me. His toy was a pair of tall leather boots, which he would rip apart as though they were paper as he watched me. Eventually, we were on our way to Boy Scout Camp in the back of a pick-up truck.

The name of the camp was Pellissippi, like the town where it was located and the State of Tennessee maintained it for the Boy Scouts. Here, I was introduced to box hockey with no reprimands for the noise it created, and a pool that floated, with a bottom. We were required to demonstrate our swimming abilities before venturing into the 250-foot deep lake waters. The lake was nearly a mile wide. After the test, we were to earn a merit badge for exploring, by rowing rubber rafts to an island some distance from the camp, spend the night, and return for breakfast next day. We felt really grownup now!

We were all good swimmers, as we had learned to swim in a stream near our home, where we pulled clumps of Bermuda grass from the banks and stacked it across a stream to create a dam. If you could stand the cold, the water became as deep as we needed. It was fifty years later that, I learned that this stream originated in the town dump and is, to this day, condemned to touch. Many things can probably be attributed to that water. I did wonder why there was never any cottonmouth water moccasins in that stream. I guess they were the smarter species!

We arrived on the island and were getting our sleeping bags ready when Lyle Olar, a kid who lived near me, started yelling at a very large yacht. He had climbed onto a rock and was yelling the only nautical words he knew, I'm sure, "ship ahoy!" To everyone's surprise, the yacht stopped and the crew spotted Lyle with their searchlight and they began yelling back for him to stay there and that they would help him. The yacht was slowly making its way through the rocks when we all began to run. The ship's crew saw this and promptly backed out, emitting language that was terrible for innocent scouts to hear!

Next morning we were up before dawn preparing to return to camp for breakfast, when Lyle didn't show. He had placed his sleeping bag near the water on a large, smooth rock and would not get up. Finally, somebody noticed why! A large cottonmouth had slept on his chest for some time. Lyle knew that the snake was there and he also knew that, while these snakes don't want to bother with a person, they would attack viciously if they decide to fight. We made some noises that caused the snake to crawl off his chest and then we were on our way.

Lyle's dedication to our trip's success was not yet complete! As we reached the rocky shore near our camp, I used my paddle to hold the boat against shore while everyone else departed. We all had packs on our backs. After all had left, Lyle held the bowline to let me jump off. Well, he almost did; when I tried to propel myself off the boat, I stayed where I was, and the boat flew out into the lake. I was sinking fast because of the weight and I began to panic as I shed the pack straps and started to climb the rocks. My lungs were filling with water because I had not been prepared for this. I surfaced to Lyle's big smile and with only one shoe. The camp staff supplied me with a new pair of Indian moccasins that I had to assemble. I lost my sleeping bag and clothes.

I still enjoyed and remember Camp Pellissippi. When I was in the Army, Lyle enlisted in the Air Force and, on a visit to the Grand Canyon, while rolling a large rock into the canyon, he and a friend fell to their death.

My brother L.C. purchased a service station and hired me to work there.. I enjoyed working there after school and after completing three paper routes, and also on Saturday and Sunday. L.C. was twenty years old, and he was dating a wonderful girl who later became my sister-in-law. Now that I was sixteen, he would allow me to operate the service station and take care of all the business by myself. I enjoyed meeting the customers, and I was very proud of his confidence in me.

A Deputy Sheriff that lived close to my parents had a beautiful yellow, convertible roadster, complete with chrome side-mirrors, engine-vent doors and radiator/grille. It also had chrome wire wheels and a giant swan, with wings spread, on the radiator cap. Sometimes, wearing his best hat, he would drive that car through town and it was really something to see.

One day, a short time after arriving home from Pellissippi, I was working at the service station, when I heard a series of "pops", which sounded like muffled firecracker reports. Then, I saw a car with two flat tires, slowly driving toward me, followed by an equally slow police car with its siren wailing, and giving chase. Because of the flat tires, the chase resembled a staged comedy, as the speed was so slow. Standing on the running board of the sheriff's car, with his left arm extended through the window, to hold himself onto the car, was the deputy. In his right hand, he held his pistol, and he was firing at the car in front of him. As they passed me, I stood against the side of the building, but still had my head exposed, so I could watch the action. The deputy continued shooting at the car ahead and both vehicles soon disappeared from sight. Later, I learned that the chase went on for another ten miles, where the deputy suffered heart failure, and died. I worked at the station until I left for military duties. I have often wondered what happened to that beautiful car.

The Fustest with the Mostest

When I was only 16 years old, I joined Company "K", 278th Infantry, (Regimental Combat Team), Tennessee Army National Guard, to be with my friends. The slogan "The Fustest with the Mostest" was adapted from the words of a Confederate General, speaking of his battle strategy. In September 1950, because of the Korean War, we were ordered to active duty at Fort Devens, Massachusetts. Being new to the active military and naïve 18-year-olds, we all volunteered when asked to do a job. We were from the "Volunteer State", home of Alvin York, but we soon became smart and stopped volunteering. "Sure, I'll volunteer for that!" was one reaction that would soon be scarce. We learned fast!

Our first training classes were on communism and communistic ideals and governments. We learned about enemies we didn't understand. Then we studied chemical, biological and radiological (CBR) warfare. We studied light infantry weapons until we could disassemble and reassemble them while blindfolded. We studied anti-aircraft artillery deployment using 105mm and 155mm weapons. We went on field trips to learn first hand how Navy artillery and Air Force aircraft operated and how to guide their fire. We studied and practiced hand to hand combat, knife training and creative weaponry (literally sticks and stones), from piano wire to pencils. We practiced day and night, hot and cold, wet and dry, snow and sand, desert and mountain combat. We trained in specially built towns and also in cliff operations. All had their peculiar requirements of special techniques and procedures of combat.

Our Unit was constantly reinforced to full regimental, now called brigade, strength of approximately 5,000 troops; about 75% new recruits, and sent through the training again and again. Each time we completed the segment, new recruits would arrive and we would do it all over again.

When we advanced to the "Maneuver", or mock combat stage, Pine Camp (soon to be renamed Fort Drum) surely looked like a battleground. Many people died in training, all from the opposing units, usually the 81st Airborne. Three C-119 "flying boxcar" aircraft, used to carry troops for parachuting lay alongside the runway in various states of destruction. In the summer training, an Army train hit a troop carrier truck loaded with troops, and many were killed. Tanks operating at night almost ran over some troops and did run over my ammo bearer's boot. I have never been so mosquito-bitten, tired, cold, hot, wet, hungry, homesick, or mentally devastated as during my visits to Pine Camp.

At Pine Camp, we also participated in a maneuver called "Operation Snowfall" during the winter of 1951, where my unit was the "aggressor" or enemy forces to the 81st Airborne Infantry. Our 5,000 men won the battle against their 50,000 troops. All I wanted was hot food and a barracks with hot water, a dry, warm bed and clean clothes.

In the spring of 1952 the big Russian tanks were pushing the Marines out of Korea, because the Marines' small "bazooka" anti-tank weapons could not penetrate the thick armor of the Russian tanks. We made out "Powers of Attorney" and our wills, and were given last rites of the church. I traveled to Haverhill, Massachusetts, to see my girlfriend Marie for the final time. However, after arriving at the airport, we were informed that the Marines had been equipped with the new 3.5 inch "bazooka" and that it worked well against the tanks. We returned to Fort Devens and the regiment was broken into small, half-battalion units and sent to various places. Some were sent to Iceland, some to Korea and I, because less than six months remained on my enlistment, was sent to Pine Camp again! This time I would await the end of my commitment, which had been extended from the initial one-year promise. Two days before my 20th birthday I would be discharged, at the new Fort Drum, having served three years, two months and twenty-eight days of my "one year" active duty assignment.

One of the people, with whom I grew up, would later have a profound impact on my life. He was a Cherokee Indian who, through high school, tried to learn all he could about his heritage. He studied Indian tradition, their holidays and researched the meanings of body-paint. Of all the people I knew, he was the most independent. Some would call him "different"! When we arrived at Fort Devens, Massachusetts to begin our full time military career, he was placed in my squad and under my command because I could understand his actions more than most. He and I became target knife-throwers. We were good! We practiced, at least twice each week, and discussed our heritage.

One morning, when we were all dressed in field uniforms, with backpacks and weapons, we had a few minutes before being called, by the First Sergeant, to "fall-in" or assemble. Jimmy was sitting on the foot of his bunk, with one foot resting on his footlocker. He teased our sergeant by saying that he was going to shoot himself in the foot. Upon this announcement he aimed, pulled the trigger and everyone heard the loud report of an M-1 Carbine doing what it was built to do. Somehow, a live round had found its way into the chamber and Jimmy turned to me and said, "I've shot myself!"

Jimmy went to the hospital and many months of healing and medical leave had removed him from my thoughts, until I was leaving post on a pass. I was traveling by bus through the North gate near the hospital, when the MPs, (Military Police), boarded the bus to routinely check for proper passes. When the MP asked the person two seats ahead of me for his ID card, he also asked his name. I heard my name, loud and clear! Jimmy had stolen, (borrowed, he called it), my identification card and permanent pass. We were both extremely lucky that the MPs turned and departed the bus before asking for my card.

Later, Jimmy went AWOL (absent without leave), and was arrested. I was sent to the base jail to determine what the problem was. When I arrived, I showed my authorization and was escorted, very seriously, through a series of gates to the cell where Jimmy was kept. He talked like James Cagney to the Military Police, and acted as if he were a hardened criminal. I'm sure I could have taken him with me if he hadn't behaved in that manner. Later though, he did rejoin the Company and was placed back in my squad. I was called to the Commander's Office and told that he had best straighten out soon!

Later, on a Friday night, I was getting ready for Saturday's routine inspection, when Jimmy came to me and asked for a favor. He had told his girlfriend's friend that if she would accompany his girlfriend to the Fort to see him, he would find a blond, blue-eyed soldier to escort her. I didn't want to stop my preparations for inspection and refused. He left, then returned, saying that he couldn't find anyone else and he asked me again to escort this lady, just for a couple of hours. I reluctantly accepted!

Marie Anne DeSesa and I walked for a while and she told me that she was to meet her friend just outside the main gate, at the bus station. I hailed a cab and, because I did not have a pass, I had intended to get out of the cab when the MP stopped it at the main gate. However, for the first time in all my rides through the gate, the MP waved the cab through and suddenly I was off base without leave, AWOL, a major offense! After saying goodbye to Marie, I began my walk back to the main gate and to the first day of my new life as a criminal, hoping they would understand. Just then, a prisoner escaped from the base prison and, as the siren sounded, the gates closed! All entering and exiting vehicles were now being emptied and checked and all people were asked for identification. I was doomed! Knowing that I would be whisked off to prison, I walked up to a guard. Exactly then, Jimmy walked from the opposite direction and started a heated conversation with the MP. As I walked slowly through the gate to safety and good citizenship, Jimmy was taken away. No one questioned me! Jimmy knew that I didn't have a pass and had caused a diversion. He was released from custody shortly thereafter.

I don't know why Jimmy didn't marry the girl he courted while at Fort Devens. All of our Company was eventually separated, and individuals were sent to various places. I lost track of everyone. Later, after returning to civilian life, I learned that Jimmy had found someone else but, on the way to their wedding, his bride had been killed in an auto accident. Later Jimmy was found in a ditch, overdosed on drugs, a tragic end to an unusual, but treasured, friend.

I tried to forget Marie. As a matter of fact, I hadn't been serious at all. She just kept entering my thoughts, even though I received a letter most every day from my girlfriend back home, who I adored. I felt like a traitor to her and couldn't understand my own actions or feelings, but I wanted to walk and talk with Marie again. I finally composed and mailed my last letter to my friend in Tennessee. I began seeing more of Marie and began to relax more each time I met her. We talked! She was frugal where I was not. She was serious where I had not been lately. She knew where her life was headed and I had stopped planning mine, because I could not become a pilot, and that was the direction in which I had wanted my life to go. I had given up! Pilot training required a college education and, although I had completed many courses through the Armed Forces Institute, they were not nearly enough!

I fell in love with Marie and hitchhiked the thirty miles each way, on Wednesday and Friday night and Saturday mornings, to see her for the remainder of my tour. She also took me to Salisbury beach in Massachusetts in 1951, where I met a, soon to be, profound partner in my life. This partner is beautiful and fascinating and sweet, but with a mind of her own. Her name is Atlantic. I had never seen an ocean before. I was eighteen and today, at 73, I am still fascinated by her. I was and still am respectful of her but absolutely in love with her. I could never leave her.

Marie's father was born in Italy and I think he was the first person that I ever met, who had been born in a foreign land, a foreign society and indeed, a foreign world. I believe that we had a mutual need for one another as we spent a lot of time together, asking each other about our childhood and what life was like growing up in our respective countries. He was a fabulous chef! He corrupted my life by introducing me to spaghetti, lasagna and ravioli, not to mention cannoli. On Sunday morning, the kitchen belonged to him and he introduced me to foods that I had never known. After Marie and I were married, he took me to his beloved Boston, where he was well known and where his brothers still lived, and introduced me to every bakery owner in the North End, as his "Rebel son-in-law"!

While in the mortar section of Company "K", the 278th Regimental Combat team, I was appointed squad leader. That was to be my first "command". My friend, Peter Morse was assigned leader of the second squad. I don't know when I met Pete; he just appeared from somewhere in my town. We must have gone to school together but I have no recollection of him. Pete talked so slowly that even Southerners lost their patience. He however, added some, well no, a lot of pepper to the conversations. He swore badly! Every sentence that he started was preceded with God's name. He had absolutely no finesse'. He went to great lengths to "tell you like it is". He was the only true segregationist I have ever known and he was proud of it.

The Army was still segregated when we arrived at Fort Devens, with blacks being assigned to the Transportation Section of our Unit. As a matter of fact, from the Company Commander all the way to the lowest driver, they were all black. One day they were marching past our barracks and Pete opened the window and called them the "N" word as loud as he could. The Commander stopped and had words with Pete, which was always ill advised. Next thing we knew, our area was overrun with angry people and a fight ensued. Most of the people from our Company didn't know what was happening, however, they were fighting in self-defense. Soon, at the direction of the Military Police, the fire department sprayed everyone down with high-powered water hoses. Even with all his faults though, Pete protected my backside from trouble many times. He would go to great lengths to see that my squad fared well when I could not be there, and I would do the same for him. We became close friends despite his (and my) shortcomings and remained so throughout our enlistment. I lost track of Pete after the service and did not hear of him for nearly fifty years when I found that he had died. Now, for the surprise! Pete went to college after the service and became, of all things, an English professor at the University of Tennessee!

We were often sent to nearby towns to march in their parades. When marching in a parade in South Boston, people found we were from Tennessee and started poking fun at the way we talked. Pete, plus a few more hot-tempered fools, raised the ante a little until a full-blown verbal battle ensued. Objects began to fly and in a short time, our Company Commander had the troops "fix bayonets" in a serious threat of defense. Boston police arrived and handled the civilians as we marched away.

Another squad leader in my Section was a German Jew who grew up with Ann Frank as a playmate. In his early teens, he was captured by the Nazis three times, having escaped each time. The last time, as he was being transported to a concentration camp, he escaped from a truck and hid in a cabbage patch. Later, his heart beat wildly as he heard voices approaching, but discovered that they were Allies. He learned that he could get his American citizenship in half the time if he joined the American Army and so he did. That's how we met.

We became close friends. He was sent to a nuclear test project in Nevada, and told me that he could see the bones in his fingers with the x-rays from the blast. We were separated when he was transferred to Iceland and I was transferred from the Unit. Many years later, I tried to find Ed while I had pilot rest time in New York. I called many, many "Goldbergs". I contacted one lady who said that she was Mrs. Ed Goldberg and that he had been in the Army at that time, and that he had died of radiation poisoning many years later. She was so convincing that I dropped my search. Forty-eight years after our military meeting, with my p/c, I found an Ed Goldberg address in Sag Harbor, Long Island, New York. I called and immediately knew I had found him. I recognized his voice instantly. We laughed and (at least I) cried for a while as he told me that he had also been looking for me. Many years before, he had driven to Kingsport, Tennessee and a service station attendant had referred him to some distant cousin of mine. He had told Ed that I was in Boston, probably meaning "the Boston area", and they were right.

Finding a Hurley in Boston is almost as inviting as searching for a Goldberg in New York. Now, however, we communicate frequently by phone and computer. We met again last year in New York State and we are planning again for this winter. He just celebrated his seventy-seventh birthday! He called me last night. Fifty-five years, and still friends.

In that icy spring of 1952, I was transferred to the 81st Airborne Infantry to await discharge at Fort Drum, where the 278th had participated in "Operation Snowfall" in 1951. I was assigned the duty of testing equipment while awaiting my release from active duty in July. Because we were now scattered around the world, I lost track of all my friends in the 278th Infantry.

I was issued a new GMC automatic drive 6 X 6 truck on which to run tests. I met another driver who ironically, had made his civilian home in the little New Hampshire town where I would later live and retire! For his heroic actions in combat in Korea, "private" Ozzie had received a "battlefield" commission as an infantry captain. That meant that he would retire at the rank of captain, no matter that he had since been demoted to private. A rule that would stand him in good stead later, many times!

Ozzie made being stationed at Fort Drum almost worthwhile. My first introduction to his "expertise" came when the motor pool needed stones to fill a deep trench that would eventually serve as a drain for the new truck-wash being constructed. Ozzie had an older truck, and we were to have the trucks loaded by hand, by prisoners. When we brought the first load, I backed my truck up to a spot perpendicular to the ten-foot deep ditch that had been dug, with the tailgate hanging over the edge. I got out of the truck and unlocked the tailgate, and the prisoners started to unload the rocks. Ozzie objected to this laborious task and proceeded to show me how to do it. He placed his truck alongside mine and drew a line in the dirt, just under the mirror. Then he pulled forward, unlocked his tailgate and his truck roared rearward toward the trench. As the mirror became aligned with the mark in the dirt, he applied the breaks hard, but the heavily loaded truck kept on going, right into the hole! The only evidence that the truck was in the site was a bumper, slightly visible above the level area where my trucked was parked. A tank retriever, a wrecker for tanks, was used to remove the truck from the trench.

Fort Drum covers such a large area, that a few small towns exists within its boundaries. They were named after towns and cities in Europe, such as Antwerp and Belgium and a few more that I cannot recall. One day we were called to help after the "tracer" bullets being fired from the fifty caliber machine guns had set the fields on fire. Tanks had been traveling in these fields after a rain, and had left deep ditches where their tracks had sunken into the soft sand. Our assignment was to pull these civilian fire engines across the fields to the fire location. I was first to get my truck attached to the little fire engine allocated to me and I started pulling it into and out of these ruts, very slowly. Ozzie passed me at a high rate of speed with parts falling of the engine. When he arrived at the fire, his fire truck was unusable.

On another occasion Ozzie sold the gasoline that was supposed to go into the "enemy" tanks to a local service station operator, and brought the truck, that we had "captured", back empty. He was court-martialed again, and his sentence was to paint the interior of a mess hall. He spray painted everything, stoves, ceilings, refrigerators, tables and windows, all white. This time he was sentenced to mop the hospital entrance floor. He mopped it with molasses he "borrowed" from a mess hall.

Upon our return to Fort Drum from an ammunitions supply trip to mid-state, New York, Ozzie had a disagreement with a motor pool sergeant.

When the sergeant ordered him to unhook the trailer containing the ammunition from his truck, he did it, intentionally, without first setting the brakes. The trailer flipped end over end as it toppled down a hill, dropping its cargo all the way down.

Long after I was discharged, I read that Ozzie had been traveling at a high rate of speed down a street that had a chain-link fence across its end. It took quite a while to extricate him from his wrapped-up convertible. I have never heard from him again and I have tried to find him, but I will always remember my last few weeks in the Army with a smile.

When I was discharged, I traveled home to Tennessee to think things over while I visited with my family and saw all my friends, including Jo, my old girlfriend. One day I was sitting on our front porch swing with my mother, having one of our talks, when I told her that I had made up my mind, that I was going to return to Massachusetts to marry Marie. Mom was very happy and asked me a lot of questions, as she had never seen Marie.

I returned to Massachusetts to find Marie's family in the middle of a move to a new home they had purchased in New Hampshire, just over the state line. The wedding date had been set a few weeks away and I shared a room upstairs, with her father. That was a big mistake! Many nights I had to go outside to get away from his stories. He told me about all the things that had happened to him while he was growing up in Italy, New York and Boston. I found that there can definitely be pain in laughter. He was the funniest man I have ever known. We did have one thing that we disagreed on. He was devout Roman Catholic and I was a devout Southern Baptist. Marie and I would be married by a Justice of the Peace, because I would not agree to raise my children as Roman Catholics. He was so stubborn that he did not attend our wedding, or the reception. I never told anyone, but I admired him for standing his ground, and I think he thought the same of me. We remained very close friends until his death. He was always very kind to me.

March 12, 1953 was a major milestone in my life! On a cool, crystal clear, spring day our beautiful baby Roxanne entered into this world in Haverhill, Massachusetts. She was the perfect addition to our world and over fifty years later I still adore her. She has presented us with two perfect granddaughters and we now have one great-granddaughter and a great-grandson who have stolen our hearts.

I had held a job as a shoe-worker and lathe operator. One day I lost my job that I had taken in a small factory. This came at a terrible time because we had sold our car to raise money to attend flight training. I had been approved for Veterans benefits totaling 75% of the flight training and I had visited the school in Revere, Massachusetts and was scheduled to attend immediately. The loss of this job was therefore devastating. We moved to Tennessee in the fall of 1954 where I would work as an apprentice ironworker with my father as my supervisor.

Fort Rucker

In 1955, while living in Tennessee, I worked as a welder in a factory where my father was a supervisor. I loved the work, but working in steel was not the cleanest work I could think of, and the pay would always be factory worker's pay. I waited for my father to pick me up each morning, at the foot of our hill, in front of the auto dealership, Brooks Motors. One morning, State Senator Carroll Brooks, the owner of the dealership, asked me what I planned to do with my life. I explained to him that I had always wanted to be a military pilot, but that it required a college education, which I could not afford. Now, although the requirement of a college education had been lifted, there was the requisite that I must be single, and I was married with a child.

The Senator seemed to be surprised at the requirement and said that he would look further into this aspect. I forgot about the conversation, as I really didn't expect anything. Soon however, a soldier came to my house to talk. He said that, because of my previous training, the military wanted me for a top-secret assignment, that I could write home every six months, but could hear from home only once a year. He said that I would be living in a foreign, unfriendly country. Of course I flatly rejected this offer. He then asked me to go to see the local recruiter and identify myself, that he had some information on a Military Flight School for me. I couldn't get to the recruiter fast enough!

I was presented with an offer to attend Army course # 6-E-33, Army Aviator Flight Training, for thirty-nine weeks in Fort Rucker, Alabama, and after completion I would be commissioned a 2nd lieutenant. Marie and our two-year-old daughter Roxanne returned to Massachusetts to stay with her mother until I was settled, at which time, they would join me. We were ecstatic!

The following morning, I was taken by bus to Fort Jackson, South Carolina, and placed in a "Re-assignment Company" in the 101st Airborne Infantry Division, "The Screaming Eagles", famous for the "Battle of The Bulge" in WWII. Everyone in this company was a veteran awaiting further duty elsewhere. Let me be the first to tell you, I felt sorry for the people who were assigned the impossible task of maintaining discipline here. We were loaded into trucks to go on work, or "keep busy" details. Each stop sign, which is every block on an Army base, found more pedestrians standing on the sidewalk after the truck left, than were there when the truck arrived. Once, a "shave-tail" (new), lieutenant was put in charge of about a dozen of us to rearrange some red, white, and blue rocks. He gave a speech before the detail informing us that this would be practiced until we were disciplined. We were to take a red rock to the top of the hill, come back and pick up a white rock and take it to the top then bring the red rock back before we could take the blue rock and start the whole process again! He informed us that he would be watching every step. I took a red rock up, then I returned for the white rock. That was delivered slightly over the top of the hill, and I was not seen on the base until the next day. This make-work project was not offered the next day. As a true Tennesseean, I wanted to volunteer.

I had asked Marie to join me there because it was a boring assignment. Every morning at four o'clock, those crazy people in the infantry companies had the new recruits marching to the beat of a drum. My paychecks were far between and the dollars were few. The allotment for my wife and child would not be paid to me for months to come. When my wife and daughter came, we walked the streets of Columbia, South Carolina looking for an apartment for so long, that they both had blisters on their feet. Marie walked barefoot and I carried Roxanne.

We found apartments, but I had not been promoted to the promised school grade of sergeant yet, and the people would not rent to a military family if the soldier did not hold the rank of sergeant, or above. However, my wife rented a room in a hotel as a civilian, not connected to the military, where she stayed and I joined her each day until we transferred to Alabama. Same people, different title! I guess they never caught on and we got the last laugh.

We rode a bus from Fort Jackson, South Carolina to Fort Rucker, Alabama. We traveled though soybean, peanut and cotton fields and many tiny towns. We were on a narrow road, traveling through a swampy area, when someone flagged the bus down. The bus stopped and a shabbily dressed black man got on. He paid his fare and the driver continued on, watching through his wide overhead mirror. As the old man made his way, he stopped in front, and to the right of our seat and sat down. The bus driver yelled at him to keep going to the rear. The old man said, "President Eisenhower said that I could sit anywhere I want!" The bus driver stopped the bus and took a wrench from the glove compartment and answered, "President Eisenhower is not driving this bus!" The old man went to the back and the bus continued on its way. My wife had never seen such prejudicial treatment before and neither had I, even though I had been raised in the segregated South.

I reported to the personnel office of the Army's Aviation School, with the sound of airplanes and helicopters everywhere. It was wonderful that I was there! I walked into the office while my wife and daughter waited outside. I was told that I would be there for eight weeks, and therefore would be in the transient barracks! I answered that he was mistaken, that I was here for thirty-nine weeks of pilot training. The clerk said, "No, soldier; you are to attend course number 6-E-33, Flight Simulator Operator and Maintenance course." I was devastated!

As helicopters flew over our heads in close formation, I took my wife and child to the guesthouse. I remarked that, in my opinion, they were flying too close to one another. I could not and cannot, after fifty years, and aviation career, see any point in that. I arrived at the guesthouse and was immediately called back to the check-in point to serve as crash area police. We picked up parts of bodies mixed with parts of helicopters from that group. Two of the helicopters had collided over tall pine trees in a swamp. I watched as a tank with a giant blade cut trees, then scooped up helicopter parts and buried them in the swamp. I had never witnessed such a waste of money as the engines, looking highly salvageable, were buried along with the rest of the aircraft while still warm from use.

I found my family a place in a town called Enterprise, Alabama. There was a monument to the boll weevil in the center of the town, with a plaque that read something to the effect that, the area had grown cotton until the boll weevil wiped out the crops. Then the farmers had switched to growing peanuts, which proved to be a more lucrative crop, hence the monument! Once while we lived there, a warehouse that housed the thin covering on the peanut kernel caught fire. The whole town smelled like peanuts for weeks!

I settled down to attending the simulator course while I thought about my situation. Meanwhile my friend Stanley Lemon had written a letter to me asking how I liked the course, as he was thinking of signing up for the same course. I wrote back, telling him of the situation, and asking him to attain and send the papers from the Recruiter's Office, if he could possible get a copy. Stanley began visiting the Recruiter every morning, bringing coffee and doughnuts. Each day he arrived on schedule, until one day he arrived without the coffee. He said to the recruiter, "I buy coffee all the time. I thought it time that you bought, for a change!" So the recruiter left Stanley in the office while he went for coffee. That was all the time Stanley needed to retrieve the forged papers that had been used to send me to a school that did not exist. He sent them directly to me.

After Stanley arrived at the school, I asked him why he had accepted the same school, knowing that the offer was erroneous and deceptive. He replied that he was not a prior service soldier and it made no difference to him.

Incidentally, he was offered the job of Commander's driver, in lieu of school attendance, which he accepted. Stanley had saved my life! Now, I had the ammunition. There, in beautiful print, on the Army Recruiter's letterhead, was the course information used to get me here. By now I was in deep financial trouble as I had two mouths to feed and for some reason, the Army could not get the allotment for my dependents started.

I wrote a letter to the Adjutant General in Washington explaining both my financial and enlistment situation. I took it to my Company Commander and asked him to sign it. He promptly told me that he was going to retire in the spring, and that I was to "make no waves". He would not sign this letter! I asked for permission to see the Inspector General, which he promptly denied. However, I went to see the Inspector General anyway, and the IG told me that I couldn't fight city hall. With that, I lost my temper and pushed the books off his desk onto the floor. He had me placed under barracks arrest. This arrest had one of my fellow students holding an empty gun on me while I slept. Then, I would hold the gun and he caught a few winks. I believe that that process is designed to be more of a scare tactic than a disciplinary method. It only served to make me angrier. Veterans have "been there, done that" and don't scare easily.

I was put on grease pit detail! All of the grease from the mess hall kitchen is captured in one deep concrete pit. I was ordered to wade into and clean out the pit, which I did. When the Company Commander stopped by to ask if I had had enough, I informed him that I was a veteran and had learned not to be afraid of my seniors. I told him that I would eventually get out of the pit! He then released me from that duty.

I was allowed to go to see my wife in Enterprise, and I had her sign the letter. The next morning I went to the orderly room and told the Commander that, if he didn't sign my letter, my wife had a copy to send for herself. He had no control over her. He signed the letter and gave me a direct order to not allow my wife to mail her copy, which I would obey.

I started the Army Instrument Flying Instructor's Course at Fort Rucker, Alabama soon after New Year's Day in 1956. All the students were veterans or re-enlistees except one, a Private Vogal! This lone inexperienced recruit was appointed as the Class Commander. I'm not sure whether it was to punish us for re-enlisting or to mentally elevate Vogal to a higher status, making him feel more equal. Whatever the reason, it proved catastrophic. We knew that as military personnel we had to march to class as a unit. However, Vogal let his command position go to his head and soon he was marching his charges in close-order drill. This frequently occurred when we were supposed to be studying, or released from duty, and our patience began to wear thin.

Because Fort Rucker was the Army's Aviation Headquarters, we were constantly paraded for review by visiting military and civilian dignitaries. One such day was very blustery! Blowing dried grass clumps rolled across the parade ground, helped along by new pilots showing their stuff in hovering helicopters. Class Commander Vogal strutted proudly alongside his troops as we joined the parade, which was being held directly in front of the Base Headquarters reviewing stand. Cannons were fired in salute, belching balls of flaming "wadding" out of their barrels and onto the dead grass, igniting our great joy, along with the dead grass. It soon was a terribly fiery scene and high-ranking dignitaries ran from the platform swatting at the burning firestorm. The helicopter pilots were looking straight ahead for traffic separation and didn't look beneath them where their downwash was fanning and spreading the flaming fury. Fire engines sped around the field, spraying water from their cab-mounted nozzles. Troops were given orders to "double-time" (run) off the field to safety. This was our chance to get even with Vogal for his exhibited prowess as drill instructor. We quickly passed the word to ignore any further commands from Vogal. Soon, the command "quick-time" was given which, in normal situations, would have immediately changed our speed to normal stride and frequency. However, we kept on running at double-time down the streets, right through the main entrance gate and into the small town immediately outside the base. Considering the chaos, the gate guard's report of troops departing the base in force, and without proper passes, was probably given a low priority. The troops decided to partake of cheeseburgers and cokes at the local diner while Vogal tried to regain control.

After lunch, we formed as a unit again and Vogal shouted "forward march". We went back to "double time" and ran right back through the entrance gate while the Military Police guard watched in total shock. We ran to our barracks, with Vogal following and yelling commands, and we dismissed ourselves from duty. I am sure that Vogal's aberration of command was not reported because we received no punishment, nor was the famous U.S. Army Aviation School's illustrious "Fireball Parade Incident" ever mentioned again. I will never write about it again. I will now destroy my p/c!

When training to be an instructor, we utilized the very first "synthetic trainers" (flight simulators), which were manufactured by the Link Company of Binghamton, New York. These devices were designated ANT-18s, for Army-Navy Trainers and they had small fuselages with wings and tail assemblies that contributed nothing to their operation. The student would get into the cockpit and close the door, then a canopy constructed from solid wood was closed over his head and the trainer was released from the straps that stabilized it. Now through hundreds of valves controlling atmospheric relations to vacuum and other experiments, he would try to maneuver the craft as if in flight. He would feel as if he were flying and the trainer transmitted its position to a recorder that resembled a large spider, which moved over the top of the instructor's desk, marking its course in red ink on plastic sheets covering a map.

The Instructor's desk faced the trainer with the Instructor's back to the aisle. The top of the desk represented North and if the trainer traveled north, the spider traveled north. Then, when the trainer turned, the spider turned, marking the course for a record of the 'flight'! The Instructor wore a headset so that he could communicate with the student. Approximately fifty of these synthetic trainers, called "Links" from their inventor's name, lined the floor of the large building.

The business offices were located on one end of the building while the rest rooms and the classrooms were on the opposite end. A girl who worked in the office had the most beautiful figure imaginable. Each time she walked from the business offices to the powder room, there was catastrophe!

Word passed quickly throughout the trainers and the hoods would open ever so slightly, then all the pilots would head their craft toward the business office and begin a slow turn to the right while this lovely goddess walked the two hundred foot length of the aisle. Because all the Instructor's maps were the same and all the students were on the same exercise, the "spiders", all fifty of them, crashed off the edge of the table at the same time, and fell with little grace onto the cement floor breaking some of them into many pieces. With the diverted attention, many trainers entered the dreaded "dead man's spiral" at this time, as their pilots lost control. I often hoped that this lady disliked her job location, because she was transferred to another building and the U.S. Army's Synthetic Flight Trainers could safely navigate again.

I had sent Marie home again to await my fate in our new "duty base" assignment. One the morning of my graduation from the Instructor's course, a sergeant interrupted the proceedings to take me to see the Base Commander. I reported and the General told me that the Adjutant General's Office, in Washington had contacted him and that I had been given three choices. They were, 1- to go "unassigned" (which is giving the Army a free hand with me), or 2- to go to Germany as an Instructor (which is no improvement), or 3- to be released within twenty-four hours with full back pay and no enlistment commitments. The latter came with permission to sue the government for damages to my family and I. I couldn't believe what I was hearing.

Shocked and confused with the rapidity and range of this development, I asked the General how much time I had to make a decision, and asked for permission to call my wife. At first he said "No", but after I explained that this was my career, he called Washington and, on hanging up the phone, he said, "Those people are eating now, you have one hour!" I rushed back to school and talked to Mr. Frank Week, my civilian instructor's instructor. He said, "Get out of here. Your life won't be worth a nickel once you take their choices. Once you've signed again, the Army's A.G. Office will wash their hands of you!" On that advice, I returned to the General's Office and at 0800 hours on March 3rd, 1956, I was processed out of the Army and delivered to a location, just outside the Main Gate. Discharged!

When I picked up my diploma from the school office, Mr. Week handed me a note. One of his friends, James Waller, was Supervisor of a civilian contract pilot training school, Anderson Air Activities at Malden Air Base, Missouri. On Mr. Week's recommendation, I was hired to start, at $450 a month, as a Link Trainer Instructor to Air Force Cadets and Student Officer Pilots. This amount of money was four times the amount upon which we had subsisted.

Mr. Weeks knew that the soldiers had been stealing food for my family, some from the military storage rooms and some pilfered elsewhere. The soldiers knew that the army had not yet sent the money for my dependent's housing or food. The men would show up before a weekend or a holiday with loose potatoes, onions, cans of vegetables, and fruit in their pockets making friends I would never forget. Here I am, fifty years later, still thinking of them and how much they meant to my family and to me. I wonder if they know!

I needed a ride home to Massachusetts, so I hitchhiked to the Air Force Base in Montgomery, Alabama to see if I could catch a training flight or freighter heading toward my destination. I was given food and a place to sleep but when I awoke a sergeant apologetically told me that, because I had been discharged, I was no longer eligible to ride on military aircraft! Of course, I should have thought of that beforehand.

On the road again, I caught a ride from an old man who was pulling a new car with another vehicle for the Telephone Company. We stopped for lunch in a town that had a statue of Booker T. Washington, about whom, he was very knowledgeable. This man was not only giving me a great ride but he was also a great conversationalist. I stayed with him for a full day until we arrived someplace in North Carolina where I said goodbye, put out my thumb and was picked up by the very first car that came along.

This was a group of sailors returning to New London, Connecticut. I was a little tired and so thankful for this ride all the way to the submarine base. Just before the base, they dropped me off at the train station, which was situated alongside the river. I was wearing a "warm weather" uniform, a short sleeve shirt with no jacket, I had not been issued winter clothes, and it had begun to snow. I was very thankful to be there instead of somewhere out on a highway.

I went for a short walk to get some fresh air and watched in amazement as a man walked across the tracks to a pier extending some seventy-five feet into the river channel and began to fish. I wondered what kind of fish he was going to catch in these waters with ice chunks floating by as if they had been broken up by a ship. While there I was treated to an unusual sight, a submarine coming upstream, to the Navy Base along the river. I had never before seen a submarine. I was very close to it and noted that only two men were visible. Both men were in the conning tower.

As the submarine was just off the end of the pier, a car sped across the tracks causing the fisherman to jump backward to prevent himself from being hit. The car sailed off the pier into the water and disappeared. The sub stopped and after a few minutes men appeared in wet suits. They went into the water and after a short time brought a body to the surface. The fisherman started screaming, "That's my wife!" It seems they had argued and he had gone to this spot to fish and be alone for a while. Evidently, she had other ideas.

I took the train to South Station in Boston and, after a short subway ride to North Station, caught a "Budliner", high-speed commuter train to Haverhill and home to my little family. After a week, I caught a bus to Missouri, with stops in New York City, Washington, D.C. and Morristown, Tennessee.

The USAF Primary Pilot Training School at Malden Air Force Base, Missouri, was equipped with T-28 "Trojan" aircraft. The students consisted of cadets, a program in its final days, and student officers. Student officers were either officers who were previously commissioned, or graduates of one of the military academies.

Frequent complaints were received that the T-28s were "buzzing" the barges on the Mississippi River.. One airplane's maintenance logbook contained the words, "engine running rough"! Next morning the dripping airplane was inspected, and it was discovered that the propeller had dipped eighteen inches in water and the fuselage covering had been bent. The pilot was the son of an Air Force General. "Dad" came for a visit, after being notified by the Accident Investigation Committee and, soon, he took his dangerously adventurous son home.

I was assigned most of the students who were on notice that their services might not be needed soon, and I was given free rein to determine how to save the Air Force's investment. I don't know why I was selected for this job. One of the students, Wallace, was a good pilot but he badly needed refinement. He did the most outrageous things.

One night seven students were scheduled to go on a designated round trip, starting in Malden, Missouri and going directly to Paducah, then to Louisville, Kentucky, on to Dyersburg, Tennessee, then to Little Rock, Arkansas and finally home to Malden. Because Wallace was one of this group, I decided to go with a patrol plane, "Blue One". Their flight instructor and I, their instrument/navigation instructor, watched as students planned the trip. Then, all the aircraft took off on the first leg. Patrol planes with instructors on board would circle each checkpoint and check each student's plane through. We arrived in Dyersburg and started "loitering" or passing time, awaiting our first check-through. I needed some practice in instrument flying in the aircraft instead of in simulators and, with a hood over my face to prevent outside references, began practicing climbing and descending turns.

Soon, the first aircraft called "Blue-1, this is Red-1 at Dyersburg, 7,500 feet, over". "Roger Red-1, This is Blue-1, landing lights please!" I would see his lights and check him off, then answer, "Thank you, Sir, proceed!" I went back to my practice. When the deadline time arrived, all the aircraft had checked through, except one, Wallace! However, several minutes later, I got the call from Wallace.

"Blue-1, Red-7, at Dyersburg, 7,500 feet. Do you see me?"

"No sir, Red-7!" was my reply, giving up my exercises to ready for the trip home.

"I just passed you head-on", he said, "let me do that again." I waited, searching the sky for a T-28 with all its lights glaring, to no avail.

"You have to see me, I almost hit you!" Just then the Command Post called from the Base. It seemed that an Ozark airliner was being "attacked" by an aircraft just North of Memphis. The voice asked, "Do you have any information on that?" I'm afraid I did!

I yelled into the microphone for Wallace to go directly to Malden. We arrived a few minutes afterwards and proceeded to the briefing room where I found him looking at his chart. "What is the matter with you? You were buzzing an airliner filled with people," I said. "Well", he said, "I dropped my map into the belly of the airplane on takeoff and couldn't get it, so I tried to do the trip from memory!" He finally graduated training six months later in Texas, and he has recently retired from a major air carrier.

On another occasion, my family and I were at the local drive-in theater in our new Buick convertible. Immediately following intermission, the lights were dimmed and we were waiting for the movie to start. Suddenly, glaring lights and a roaring engine screamed between the projection house and the screen, then the bright lights went off and the intruder was gone. The next morning I was appointed, as a member of the Incident Investigation Board, to interview all who had been flying that night, to no avail.

Some ten years later, I was talking to a "new hire" pilot for Northeast Airlines over coffee and asked him where he got his training. This information would help me to understand what training may be required to make him ready for airline pilot training. He answered, "Malden, Missouri, Sir!" We talked and finally he laughingly told me of this escapade. I took his shoulder and said, "Do you remember a tall blond instructor who sat at the center of the table facing you?" He took a long, hesitant look and then we both smiled as I said, "Just like the Mounties say, George, "we always get our man, and please, don't try that with an airliner!" George later died in a hunting accident.

Grenier Air Force Base

In December, 1957, when I was advised that the Primary Contract School where I worked in Missouri, was being disbanded, I was the first to volunteer to go. We drove home to New England and I started working for the U.S. Air Force at Grenier Air Force Base in Manchester, New Hampshire. I was hired as Training Officer, (Instrument Flying Training). I was handed the keys to my office and was told that I would have any assistance I might need, otherwise, I was on my own. I remember my first lecture vividly.

The FAA, (Federal Aviation Agency), had implemented a new procedure for aircraft entering "holding patterns" and it was adopted by the Air Force. During the first week of my new job, I had to teach this new procedure to the squadron pilots. I prepared myself, I thought, rather thoroughly and proceeded to the classroom. However, when I was introduced and took the podium, I immediately felt panic! These were not eager students who would hold on to my every word. These were gray-haired men from World War II, who either slept through the class or questioned every word with a snicker. My nerves began to clog my airway with words and I had great difficulty speaking. My immediate supervisor, the Flying Training Officer, the Base/Squadron Commander and the Operations Officer sat in the front row and never said a word. My new world had crumbled. I was devastated! As I left the classroom I wondered what would become of me, and how I would tell Marie that I had failed in my new position of which we were so proud.

The Base Commander soon came to my office. He smiled and said, "Don't let them get you down. They have to answer to you!" He continued, "They were pushing you but, although they don't know it, they have to take an exam administered by you, on the subject you just covered and if they fail", he added, "they're grounded!" That afternoon, when I entered the classroom to administer the test, the Commander shook my hand and said, "Good lecture. Now don't answer any questions from these slobs!" About half of my "new" students failed the exam and were grounded, with no pay, for one month before they could even hear the lecture again. I was walking in tall cotton!

One day I noticed a lot of people, whom I did not recognize, walking around my office building. I knew that a secret aircraft, called "Puff, the Magic Dragon" was housed in a hangar next door, so I went outside and challenged their security clearance. I learned that they were news people who were awaiting the arrival of the new astronaut, Alan Shepard. When Alan finally arrived, he taxied his aircraft quickly to within a few feet of my office door. With all of those people tearing and yelling at him, he ran to my door and knocked. I let him in and immediately locked it. He introduced himself, as if everyone didn't know him. His uniform was torn and someone had even pulled his hair. Once some of the excitement subsided, we left through another door and into my car. I drove him home, which was about a mile from my own residence in Derry, New Hampshire. We continued this pattern intermittently, for about a year, and then he moved his family to Texas. I would not see him again. However, I did meet John Glenn, who had parked behind my house to hide, during Alan's celebration parade in Derry. By the time the town had arranged the parade, John had orbited the earth and didn't want to up-stage Alan who had not orbited during that first ride. Later I had the honor of having Glenn ride in my cockpit during a trip to New York City in a DC-9.

The regular Air Force departed Manchester, which changed the name of the facility from Grenier Air Force Base to Grenier Field, and the base was left to the Reserve and National Guard Forces. Colonel Gardner Mills commanded the 732nd Troop Carrier Squadron, the unit that now employed me. His duties, Base and Squadron Commander, required much diplomatic, political and social work, above and beyond the normal duties of an aviator. In addition, he had the same annual flight qualification and proficiency requirements as those of any pilot in the squadron. He asked me if I would "pencil in" his required visits to my simulator to keep him current, and he promised that he would pay me the obligation when the opportunity arose. He always paid his debt! Once, while in the simulator, he received a call from a General at the Pentagon. As I was trying to tell him of the call, I tripped on the wire, pulling the phone onto the cement floor and breaking the ceramic handset into several pieces. He exited the trainer and, while I used both of my hands, and he both of his, to hold the pieces together, he placed his face on the floor and received his Squadron's "Orders to Active Duty" from Washington, during the Cuban Missile crisis. We were laughing so hard that he had to tell the General what had happened and our present position. Much to our delight, the General laughed, too!

While working with the Air Force Troop Carrier Unit, many new pilots came off their first active duty assignment, released to the Reserves. These Reservists had to maintain the same training requirements and qualifications, and fly the same number of hours, as if they were still on active duty. One of these pilots had a family in Bradford, Pennsylvania and he asked me to fly him home to begin his vacation. I needed the flight time and he would pay for the use of the aircraft and the fuel, so the trip was planned for a Saturday morning at an early hour. At departure time, it immediately became evident that he did not understand that this aircraft was a very small, slow, civil aircraft. It could not carry passengers plus a lot of luggage. We left many of his belongings in my office, in New Hampshire and were soon on our way. The scenery was beautiful, with the typical New England and New York October color show, but we were flying into headwinds that were slowing our "ground speed" ,(progress over the earth), by forty miles per hour, almost a third of the planned speed. At this rate, I would have to make an earlier stop for fuel than I had planned.

I looked on the charts and found a small airport in Ballston Spa, New York, directly on our flight path that was listed to have food and fuel. We flew the normal "downwind" leg and looked over the grass runway, as there was no radio communication available. I made the approach, flared to land and, as the aircraft slowed to the speed where it would not fly any more, I saw the grass. It was three feet tall and the belly of the little Cessna flattened it as the wheels tore through the wheat-like growth, bringing us to a, rather sudden stop.

We went inside where we found a scenario more like an Early Tennessee country locale, than New York State. Some older people sitting around a pot-bellied stove were as surprised as we were that we had arrived. I asked, "Isn't the airport open?" "Yep! What can we do for you?" was the reply. "Well, I need fuel but first, I need someone to cut the grass so I can move the aircraft!" "Sit down!" a lady spoke up, what do you want to eat? I'll get it for you while the men cut the grass." She said. We asked for cheeseburgers and she started to light the old wood stove. We grew silent as we watched.

I walked out to watch the progress in getting the airplane freed up to get to the fuel pump. I noticed a group of men gathered around it, looking at the front end. I thought they might have found some damage, although I didn't think I had hurt the nose-gear. I walked over and asked them what they were looking at, and they explained that this was the first aircraft of that model, (a Cessna 150, with a tricycle landing gear), that had ever landed there. It set me back a bit because Cessna had manufactured that model aircraft for a few years.

We dined on the best cheeseburgers I have ever tasted. Then, saying goodbye to a wall of waving well-wishers, we took off on the newly "re-surfaced" runway. That scene became well established in my memories. More memories were ready to be made on this trip, however. I found that the airport in Bradford, Pennsylvania is situated completely within the confines of a "hairpin" turn in a river. The runway extends from bank to bank and, because there are trees on either end, causes the usable surface to be rather short. But the Cessna excels in that kind of situation. In just a few minutes I was on my way on the three-hour trip home. Now, I hoped the wind would push my airplane to add, instead of subtract speed. It didn't!

I stuck to my flight plan and landed at an airport in Elmira, New York, with commercial operations and a glider manufacturing company. The tanks were "topped off", I checked the oil etc., and I was on my way. Once I was airborne, I started talking by radio, to the "FAA, Flight Service Station" in Concord, New Hampshire. I knew all of these operators, as I had taught them instrument flying techniques and procedures at my home field. They were working a few miles north of my home. I talked for a while and I told them that I was now going to clean up the cockpit and put some things away, while on my way home. My heading was 85 degrees on the magnetic compass that included a 6-degree correction for the wind effect. Nighttime had arrived and I could see lightning flashes in the distance, on my right and left, but not directly in front of me.

I had used the transmitter and left it on "receive", turned on the "navigation" (clearance) lights, and the anti-collision (flashing red) light, then turned the cockpit flood light on to see the various charts, maps and papers in the seat beside me. After putting the charts, the paper etc. away, I noticed something very wrong. The sunset glow was right beside the propeller. "Whoa!" I thought, "The sun sets in the west, so it should be to my rear."

I noticed that the compass still indicated 85 degrees. Although the floodlight was still on, all other lights and the radio were dead and the instrument lights had gone out. I turned the aircraft immediately to place the sunglow on my tail, where it belonged. "But how long have I flown westerly and even more important, how much of a curve have I flown? How far off my planned path am I?" I wondered.

I had no idea where I was, but I could see sparse lights on the ground, so I was not near a big city. Soon the sun-glow was gone, so I had to keep finding two lights aligned with my direction and fly that course, then keep adding one more light. I hoped that I would eventually see total darkness. That would be the ocean. Then, I would look for Boston, and I knew that the controllers would clear traffic because my friends in Concord would have already alerted them. Once I identified Boston, I would know where Grenier Air Force Base and home would be. Eventually, I saw the blue-light outline of a taxiway directly beneath my wheels. I reduced power and aligned the aircraft with the paralleling runway and was ready to land when a car turned his lights on and, while shining a spotlight in my eyes, drove directly down the runway toward me. As I pulled up, I recognized the Fort Devens, Army

Airfield. Something good had eventually come out of all the nights that I had walked guard around that field some ten years earlier.

I had become somewhat concerned because all the fuel gauges indicated empty. Of course I knew that I had plenty of fuel, but nothing is more disturbing in an airplane than to have gauges indicating something that they shouldn't be indicating. It bothered me! I landed nearby at Fitchburg, Massachusetts to refuel, just to ease my mind. The attendant told me that I had forgotten to turn my lights on and I just said, "Oh, thanks!" After refueling I left for home, illegally of course, with no lights and I landed visually at Grenier Air Force Base. I put the airplane away, notified my friends at the Flight Service Station by telephone, then went home. Next day, because they were not equipped with radar at that time, I had to tell the Air Force Control Tower personnel that I had sneaked in with no lights, landed and put the airplane in the hangar without their knowledge.

Later, the mechanics found that with all the demand I had placed on the generator, a fuse had not only blown, but had welded the battery lead to the instrument panel, rendering everything electrical, except the dome light, inoperative.

Rotor Wings

In 1963, while working for the Air Force as a training officer, I wanted to increase my aviation qualifications by checking out in a military aircraft. I was presently, restricted to ground training. Although I was too old to qualify for fixed wing training, the Massachusetts Army National Guard had a helicopter training course that required membership in the National Guard unit after the schooling was completed. I applied, passed the tests, was accepted and soon was waiting for a class date, for the Warrant Officer Rotary Wing Aviator Course at Fort Wolters, Texas.

While waiting, I was sent to the Boston National Guard Armory to appear before the board, to be sworn in as an Army officer. My wife accompanied me to Boston and, as we stopped in front of the armory, a Boston policeman directed me to park elsewhere. President Kennedy was going to speak there that night and a parking ban was in effect. My wife waited in the reception area while I found a parking space elsewhere. She conversed with some military personnel who were serving as an advance party for the presidential visit. After about two hours of ceremony and the signing of papers, we returned to our home in New Hampshire.

Two very pertinent events occurred during the next few weeks of 1963. On November 22nd, President Kennedy was assassinated in Dallas, Texas, and on Friday, December 13th, I reported for Warrant Officer Candidate (WOC) Training at Fort Wolters, Texas, forty miles from Dallas. Upon arrival, we proceeded to the Base Dependant Housing Offices and were shown housing that was so dirty that I wouldn't allow my family to stay there. We decided to rent a small home close to a school for my two children, in the nearby town of Mineral Wells. Once I reported to school at 5 PM on Friday, the 13th of December, I was not allowed to see my family again, except for one hour on Friday nights and on Sundays in church. I was escorted to and from church, and back to my quarters, by two "upper classmen".

Christmas Eve was soon to come however, and my family and I spent December 23rd through New Years Day together. Training was fast and furious when it did resume. Physical exercises, running, square meals (while sitting on the first three inches of the chair), and study, filled my day. We all suffered from loss of our vocal abilities from having to scream every word, but the sound began to return within a few days. Because of my aviation instructor's training and prior infantry training, I did well on my course.

There was an announcement that an upper classman had found the murdered body, belonging to one Don D. Dudd, an upper classman, and good friend to all, in our pool- room. We were assigned relationships in his life, and had to complete a formal investigation of his death, and conduct a military trial and funeral. The deceased represented by a pair of sox, was honored with speeches and tributes (including a 21- gun salute), and interred, with full military honors, including a hearse, mourners, casket and headstone, in a military cemetery at Ft. Wolters. This activity was, shall we say, dead serious, as the Adjutant General's Office in Washington, D.C. graded each student's performance, practically and academically, as to our respective performance of duties expected of us as officers of a military unit.

We started flying immediately after the Officer Qualification. I really enjoyed the H-23 "Raven" helicopters, although they were wild machines, unlike anything I had ever imagined. There was no relaxation, even for a second, lest you unwittingly enter ugly acrobatic stages. One day while I flew from my home field to a remote field for practice, I was contacted by radio and instructed to return to the base field. On return, I was whisked to the hospital with no explanation, and was taken to a colonel's office .He informed me that my wife was sick, and that the Army had decided to send her to Ft. Hood, Texas for treatment. He said that she had been feeling strangely and had come to the Ft. Wolters Hospital and that the Red Cross would place my children in a good home, with a Texas family.

I asked to see my wife and was driven to her home, and told that I could stay with her, but that I would need to notify them the next day, as to what we had decided to do. Marie seemed well, but excitable and ironically, so were the children. She told me that someone had been in her bedroom one night, and when she awoke, he ran away before she could see his face. A neighbor had placed flour on the porch steps to see if he could find tracks and, sure enough, the next day, there were boot-tracks in the flour. Marie was very concerned, especially with the two children and her husband not at home.

After falling asleep that night, Marie awakened me and, pointing to the window, said "Someone is waving a tree limb across the window!" I tried to assure her that it was only the wind but she told me that there were no trees near that window. I went out the opposite door and surprised the person who was holding the tree limb; he dropped the limb and ran into the field. I ran after him, clad only in shorts with no shoes, across the barbed wire fence and deep into the dark, cactus littered field before I thought about where I was. It was a slow trip home.

Marie told me that she had gone to a civilian doctor, and when entering the waiting room, encountered someone familiar. She sat directly across the room from the Sergeant with whom she had had the conversation in Boston, President Kennedy's Assistant! She asked him what he was doing there and he informed her that all personnel were "frozen" in place after the president was shot. He was curious as to why she was there and she reminded him that I had been accepted to this school when she saw him in Boston.

I tried to assure her that all that was just a coincidence and told her what the base doctors had said. The next morning, I informed the Colonel that I had decided to take my family home to Massachusetts and familiar family surroundings. I was processed out of school while Marie took the car for service and got the kids' school records transferred.

I was notified in writing by the Commanding General that I would be the very first person that had ever been allowed to leave the school and return. I found that my flight grades were all "AA" except for one "A" and I had attained a 92 percentile score in the Warrant Officer Qualification Course.

Except for the local gas company, who would forward the balance of our deposit, all bills were paid in full and we started our trip to Massachusetts at about nine o'clock at night. We had only driven a few miles however, on a lonely country road when the lights began to dim. Soon, the car began to slow. As I looked for a place to pull off the road, we came upon a service station that luckily, was open. We drove in, but before the hood could be opened, the engine died. The mechanic immediately spotted the problem. Someone had loosened the generator drive belt. He tightened it, gave the battery a boost and we were again on our way. When we pulled off the highway at the service station we had both noticed a car that slowed behind us and then passed at the last moment before we stopped. The reason we had noticed this car, in particular, was that it had only one operable headlight and no other cars were on the road. It was very conspicuous as it also had long (about 5 ft) steer horns on the hood. We mentioned these unusual facts in conversation as we traveled. After we had driven for an hour or so, we decided to stop for coffee and a sandwich before everything closed. I pulled in to a diner and shortly thereafter that same car, with the steer horns and one headlight, passed the diner going the same way we had been traveling. He had somehow fallen behind us.

Now, Marie was upset with suspicions that this car was following us and I tried to calm her by saying that they probably saw our New Hampshire

Plates, were going in the same direction, and were just following us. It was a weak explanation but I was also becoming concerned. We bought coffee and sandwiches, tucked the kids away in the back seat, and resumed our travels, only to find that, within minutes, that car was behind us again. He had waited for us to leave the diner.

The car followed us for a couple of hours and I decided to try to lose him. Upon entering a small town near Greenville, Texas, near the border of Arkansas, I accelerated to high speed and left him. As soon as I lost sight of him, I took a side street, then another, and after hiding behind the buildings, turned the lights off. We lost him! But this action, painfully depicting a bad detective thriller, had upset Marie and the children, never mind me. Now, trying to use a calming voice, I made the decision that we could sleep in this deserted, unlighted parking lot for the remainder of the night. Everyone slept, feeling that we were safe for a while.

Suddenly, a loud noise interrupted the silence. A train, with its whistle blowing, had passed within a very few feet of the car. We hadn't noticed the railroad tracks barely five feet away. We drove on, entering Tennessee at Memphis, and we only had four hundred miles to travel before arriving at my parents' home in East Tennessee, to safety and rest. We felt better now, with the daylight, and could see what was happening.

We entered Knoxville, just 50 miles from my parent's home, at about ten o'clock that night, and we hadn't seen that car since we lost them near Greenville, Texas. We were low on fuel. I stopped at a service station across from the University Of Tennessee, and as I got out of the car, the attendant asked me if I could pay him in the exact amount. He told me that a man who was sitting in the office, had a pistol pointed at him, and was watching us. "This is just what I need and at the perfect time!" I thought. I looked at the man with the gun and got out enough to pay without change. The attendant asked me to notify the police. The man came out and started threatening with the gun while I drove away. Luckily, the first car I met was a police cruiser and, by flashing my headlights, I stopped them. After relaying the information, we watched them speed away to the rescue. We continued on our trip.

We arrived at my parents' home before daylight and, after a short rest, continued on. The kids had plenty of room to sleep in the car. We left in the early afternoon and crossed the Virginia state line as the sun was setting behind us. We looked forward to an uneventful trip for the remainder of our journey. But soon, in the rear-view mirror, a car with one headlight appeared. I continued driving and didn't mention it. It had been five hundred miles since we had seen it. It probably was another car anyway. But Marie, remembering our fright from the night before, cast a peek to the rear occasionally, and it was not long before she spotted it. Talking it over, I slowed and let it pass us. It was the car with the long steer horns on the hood and the driver looked directly at us. There were also other people with him. Now, this was really serious, and I was scared!

We were traveling along route U.S.11 in the Shenandoah Valley, paralleling the mountains. The Scenic Skyline Drive runs along the crest of that mountain and although treacherous, would give me a chance to lose that car. I left the main road in Natural Bridge, Virginia, followed by the driver of that one-lighted car, who knew by that time that we recognized them. I took a couple of side streets but we were still followed. We still could not figure why all this was happening. We couldn't go looking for a police station, so I had to lose him again. I reversed course quickly, and again we verified that it was the same car that had followed us from Texas.

I accelerated before he turned and, luckily, I saw a sign for the Skyline Drive. Quickly, I took it! Marie kept looking back, nearly in tears for fear for the children. My heart was pounding, but after a while with no visual contact, we felt better. No lights followed and because of the darkness, I began to feel that we could slow to a safer speed. After all, I was very tired and only half way home. I asked Marie to drive while I tried to sleep a little. In retrospect, I couldn't sleep today knowing the Skyline, even if Richard Petty was driving, but I was so tired. However, sleep never came and after a short rest, I was back behind the wheel, hoping Marie could sleep and rest.

We re-entered route U.S.11 just west of Front Royal, Virginia at the end of the Skyline Drive and stopped at the first motel we found. We got a room and were feeling pretty good until Marie looked out our window, with the room lights off, and saw the car with one headlight, park in front of a room not thirty feet from ours. Men were leaving the car and entering a room where they had an uncluttered view of ours. There were four men, dressed in long-sleeved white shirts with ties. One of them came to the closest window and looked directly toward our room. We re-packed, gathered the kids and exited in one quick swoop and while they scrambled to their car, we sped off toward the New Jersey turnpike. We were only half way through Maryland when they were behind us again. They didn't try to hide it, they were following us, and there was nothing we could do. Even if we found the police, what could they do? What would we say? Who would believe this? Under the circumstances, I wouldn't have!

We were again running low on fuel. As we entered the New Jersey Turnpike, I got an idea. I accelerated to a very high speed as they followed, close behind. Then, in a split second, I took the "service area" exit, but so did they. I immediately, and still at high speed, took the lane for "trucks" as he went into the "cars" lane and I saw his brake lights glow. Now, I accelerated to as fast a speed as I could possibly go safely and re-entered the turnpike. I never saw that car again. We still are puzzled as to why they followed us. Maybe it stemmed from the meetings in Boston first, then the doctor's office in Texas. Was it related to the assassination? Were they Secret Service personnel wondering what was going on with us? Were we suspects? We'll never know.

About a week later, the Mineral Wells Gas Company notified me that a gas leak was found in a baseboard-mounted, portable heater in the house, where Marie and the children had lived. Within a few days Marie and the kids were feeling fine, but we won't forget our trip soon.

The Commanding General of the Massachusetts National Guard sent us a letter that I could return to school as soon as I wished. However, I left the National Guard in 1964 and I continued working for the Air Force until early 1966, when I started working for Northeast, later Delta, Airlines. I never returned to helicopter school.

Out of Body

I had recently driven from Mineral Wells, near Fort Worth, Texas, to Eastern Massachusetts with only a very short stop half way, and was visiting a military friend at Pease Air Force Base, in New Hampshire, where he was based. We had decided to go to a "Big Band" concert at the Officers Club on the base. I did not have the proper attire and he loaned one of his jackets to me. It was the ugliest jacket I had ever seen. Those jackets are certainly the type you loan, and I reluctantly agreed to wear it simply because it fit me and a jacket was required for admission to the club. My wife really wanted to see the band.

We arrived at the club and entered through a reception area with a "stand up" bar, to our left, where long-stemmed cocktail glasses were stacked four high, on trays. The theater was not open, so we sat at a table in the regular bar room. As we sat and talked my legs suddenly became uncomfortable, with pain in the back of the thigh and calf of both legs. I excused myself and walked through the reception area to the entrance and continued outside into the ice-cold temperatures.

After a short walk, I returned, and again sat on the bench-type seat. The pain returned, even more intense than before. Because I did not wish to ruin the evening, I tried to ignore it but, after a few minutes, I abruptly left the table and started my return to the sidewalk to exercise my legs. The pain was excruciating! Each step was more painful than the last. I remember thinking that it felt as if my legs had been severed and I was walking on the business end of a sword. Then, I saw many glasses, broken on the floor, their tall stems now separated from their bowls and silently spinning, as my face landed directly into them.

I then felt myself floating in an opposite corner of the large reception area, near the ceiling, about ten feet above the floor, and fifteen feet away from my body, looking down. I saw my wife as she called to my body. I had no pain, no cares, and felt no emotion. As a matter of fact, I felt totally serene!

I saw my body lying lifeless on the floor below. From my position, I watched and listened as someone called for a doctor among the patrons, and attendants called for an ambulance. Two Air Force medics immediately responded and were taking my blood pressure and administering CPR. A beautiful girl in evening clothes stood above my body and laughed. The medic looked up at her and said, "This man is not drunk lady, please move!" They pumped my chest in and out, but I had no sensation. My mind was on that ugly jacket, which I still wore as I laid there, but it and my shirt had been opened to bare my chest. It was still ugly!

I watched as the medics worked feverously to regain my heartbeat, until the ambulance attendants arrived and placed my body on the stretcher. I only returned to my body after they had placed it into an icy, cold ambulance. I awoke and asked the attendant why ambulances were not kept inside on cold nights. We both had a laugh!

It was determined that I could use the Emergency Air Force Facilities because I was a civilian Air Force employee who occasionally did work on this airbase. The finding by the Air Force doctors was, because I was so slim, sitting for so long during the trip and on subsequent days, had restricted the flow of blood between my heart and legs. Then, when I stood, the blood was pulled to my legs, causing a distribution problem that eventually, affected my heart. The medics reported that my heart had stopped beating for three minutes. My body had no pulse while I was happily occupying my position in the corner of the ceiling.

Now, after many such stories, doctors agree that you can lose your heartbeat for rather long periods, during which time, many strange tales come about. Except for having to see that ugly jacket and the pain of getting there, it was a wonderful trip. I spent three minutes in heavenly paradise and something I had never even imagined; that I had no weight and no feel of gravity pulling down on me. Best of all, I can remember how great that felt! I would happily live in that state of being forever. Even today, when I think of it, I smile.

At the risk of my credibility, I will tell you about another unusual experience. I was in the U.S. Army's Rotary Wing (Helicopter) Pilot's Training School in Mineral Wells, Texas when I was 33 years old. I was to be trained for the Massachusetts Army National Guard and , after training, return to my National Guard assignment. I had the "blessings" of some high ranking Air Force Officers, because, even though the Army had trained me, I had worked for seven years for the Air Force as an Instrument Flying Instructor.

I was also 13 years senior to the average student. It was unmistakably obvious on the first day, that the cadre didn't like the idea that Air Force officers had underwritten my candidacy as an Army Warrant Officer. Although my grades were highest in the class, the cadre (training) personnel tried physically to force my withdrawal. I had previously accomplished some tough military training and I was determined that they would not impede my progress.

I slept on the floor beside my bed because of the middle of the night inspections we encountered. I had a Spanish Army student as a roommate and he also slept alongside his bunk. We were sleeping sometime in the early morning hours when I was awakened by an unusual sound and sight. I saw an extremely white, spewing light about 18 inches across, between the window and me. Inside this light there appeared the face of Jesus.

There are times in my memories that I believe something was said but now I really can't remember if that is so. It extinguished as quickly as it had appeared and I checked to see if I was awake. I was! Iglesius continued sleeping while I spent the rest of that night in my study chair.

Next morning, I was halfway between my home field and a practice field and received a radio call to return to my home field. I parked the aircraft and a car drove alongside. The driver told me that he was to take me to see the Commanding General at the Post Hospital. I was told of Marie's problems and sent to her home in Mineral Wells. Next day, we were on our way home. (See ROTOR WINGS). Before I left, I received an apology from the Officers of the Training Company for the treatment I had received. Approximately one month later, I received a personal letter from the school's Commanding General. He stated that no student had ever been allowed to return to training once it had been interrupted, and that I would be the very first candidate who would be encouraged to return to finish my training at my convenience. However, I would not return.

Aviator s Fate

A Fairchild-Hiller 227 or FH-227 is a high winged, turbo-prop aircraft that carries 44 passengers and a crew of three. That was the first aircraft that I flew for Northeast Airlines. I was based in Boston in 1967 and, because I had worked in the training department for a year, was a senior first officer even on my first trip. Because I was senior among the FH-227 first officers, I would often fly with a senior captain. Senior captains are occasionally assigned new pilots who have been recently released from training and need initial operating experience.

I had initially been hired as a Director of Training and served as an Instrument Flight Instructor (Ground Training) at my request, so that I could get used to the training method differences from the Air Force, where I had worked for 11 years. I didn't like the fact that non-rated personnel were teaching new pilots. One night, while on my way home, I returned to the office of the Vice-President, who had hired me, and gave my notice. The Vice-President offered me a seniority number as a pilot if I would stay in the Training Department for one year and help with the training bulge. I agreed and after that year of accruing seniority, was sent to train on the FH227 aircraft.

I had transferred from the Training Department to the Flight Operations Department and had gone to school with a "new hire" pilot who had been flying support for Francis Gary Powers of U-2 fame. Ray had also been a personal pilot for the Kennedy family from Massachusetts.

There were only three "students" in my class, a senior pilot, Ray and myself. I finished training and with only 6 hours in the aircraft, was released to fly the line. On my first passenger carrying flight and before my first regular schedule, the captain was being "line checked" and the check captain, noticing that I was not comfortable, asked me if I would like to go back to training, to which I answered, "Oh, yes, please!" I returned to Flight Training for one more "aircraft familiarization" flight. The next week, when I was sent to LaGuardia Airport, New York for my first scheduled trip, I had a grand total of eight hours in this type aircraft, which was my first "airline type aircraft". It was also my first jet powered aircraft and the largest aircraft I had ever flown.

Other captains didn't like the fact that Ray, who was hired only as a flight-training pilot, was sometimes ordered by the company to fly the line as captain, even though he was junior to all other captains. The first officers didn't like the fact that the company assigned me duty as his first officer on scheduled flights, because my seniority was earned in the Training Department. At most places where we landed, notes were awaiting us that nice people shouldn't read. They thought that we had not earned our status but the company sent us out together many times, anyway.

On the first day that I was totally released from training, I was assigned to LaGuardia Airport, in New York, to maintain a regular schedule for my first month. I reported to the captain in Operations at LaGuardia and he said to me, "I hope you have a lot of experience in this aircraft because this is my first trip as a captain, without a check pilot". Well, was he surprised! He was as nervous as a cat and I don't blame him.

We were notified that our aircraft had flown an earlier flight to New Bedford, Massachusetts but had returned with a "heavy vibration" and that a check pilot would take it up for further flight check before it would be released to duty. The check pilot walked in, asked me to go with him and we soon were taxiing toward the take-off runway for Long Island Sound, an area assigned for "test hops".

The check pilot put the airplane through its paces, finding nothing unusual and returned to LaGuardia to land. Just alongside the landing runway on the "downwind" leg, he said "Take over, I'm going to the back to check for vibrations." When he was in the tail of the passenger compartment, the control tower cleared me for immediate approach. I reduced the power, hoping he would come up and just then, the vibration announced itself. The propeller was violently trying to get off the engine. I knew we needed to get on the ground, fast. So I put the landing gear down and did the entire checklist that I had memorized and landed without a pilot in the captain's seat. The check pilot rolled into his seat as I was braking and stated that because of the descent and forces, he couldn't get into the cockpit. I had landed an airliner solo, at one of the busiest places in the aviation world, with only eight hours pilot time in that type aircraft.

We were given another airplane to fly to New Bedford, Massachusetts, with a return to LaGuardia. As he mentioned before, the captain was extremely unsure of his aptitude in this new aircraft. He had me saying "thank you" and "please" with every radio transmission. He was a wonderful person but extremely nervous. So was I!

One day at the end of that month, he assigned me to fly the first leg of our trip and we were beaten up by turbulence. I landed at New Bedford in 78 knots of wind, bouncing badly on contact with Mother Earth because the aircraft would fly at the same wind speed as that with which I landed. The captain took control of the aircraft after landing, as he had the only steering wheel for ground operation. When he turned the aircraft to leave the runway, we heard a loud "bang". We continued to the gate area and discharged the passengers.

New passengers were loaded and, after retrieving the paperwork, I "walked" or inspected the airplane. It seemed that everything was in order but in my mind I thought, "Something is not right." I asked the captain if I could look at the airplane again. He said, "Yes, of course!" I walked around the aircraft again without finding anything unusual and started up the stairs to the passenger compartment when something caught my eye. The landing gear doors were swinging in the wind. I returned to the wheel wells and noticed that the rods that operate the large landing gear cover doors were broken off. I called maintenance in Boston, and we were dispatched direct to Boston for repairs. We removed the passengers and the flight attendant as a mechanic removed the doors.

After storing the large doors in the passenger compartment, we departed for Boston. We had to leave the flight attendant in the operations office to await our replacement flight, because we were not allowed to take her on a now "maintenance" flight. She was crying because she was scheduled to connect to a flight in New York that would take her home to Miami. Now she had to wait for our replacement aircraft to fly her back to New York where she would probably be re-assigned another trip at the company's discretion.
Arriving in Boston, we taxied directly into the hangar. A training pilot and two students were waiting to use our aircraft for training as soon as the doors could be repaired. We successfully argued that they remain on the ground for the remainder of the day.

We were issued a new aircraft and dispatched on a "ferry" flight, with a new flight attendant, to Manchester, New Hampshire. Another FH227 had been flying to Manchester when the first officer reached for a switch that was positioned right in front of, and above, the captain's face. At the same instant, the aircraft had encountered moderate turbulence and the captain's eye tooth was loosened to the horizontal position after hooking it under the first officer's wedding ring and he was undergoing emergency dental surgery at the hospital in Manchester. We were to take his passengers to LaGuardia.

We had taken off to the northeast from Boston and immediately encountered more, now severe, turbulence caused by the strong winds. Just as I picked up the logbook to record the "gate and off" times, we hit a tremendous downdraft that threw me against the top of the cockpit ceiling, breaking the seatbelt, and cutting my scalp on the air conditioner ductwork above my seat. Apparently I was unconscious for a few minutes. I was covered with blood and when I gathered my senses, I went through the cargo area to the cabin, to check the aircraft for damage.

I found the flight attendant screaming and buried in debris, head down and covered with cushions and blankets. She couldn't see with the blanket wrapped around her head, and she thought we had all died. I placed her in a seat, buckled her in, and returned to the cockpit. The captain had started his approach to Manchester Airport, called for an ambulance, and declared an emergency, a required procedure because the aircraft only had one able crewmember. When we stopped at the gate, I stepped down into the cargo compartment, opened the cargo door and stepped out onto the tarmac only to fall flat on my face. My legs were rubber.

I was taken to the hospital with cuts and bruises, along with a concussion. Then, I was sent home to Massachusetts, by taxicab. Another pilot was sent to the New Hampshire airport, from Boston to take my place. I arrived home unscheduled and without my car. In the ensuing discussion with my wife, I decided that I was going back to the Air Force. However, after four weeks, I was pronounced, ready to fly, and returned to duty.

One rainy evening in 1967, my schedule called for me to fly from Boston to Lebanon, New Hampshire, Montpelier, Vermont, Burlington, Vermont, and return to Boston. The captain of that flight was the same captain who had had his eye tooth nearly extracted in Manchester. I had flown with him on that route many times and we were both well aware of the stories about the navigation system at Lebanon, which I had heard even before I left the Air Force. Since WWII, pilots had frequently "written-up" the low frequency radio transmitter that was used for guidance to the airport. A system in the aircraft called the ADF (automatic direction finder), causes a needle to point to that station and, because a compass card rotates directly under that needle, it shows the pilot the direction to fly to the station. This facility had been "written up" because the needle was reported to have reversed prematurely at times, indicating that the station had been passed, when indeed, it had not. However, the FAA had routinely checked the facility and no erroneous transmissions were ever found.

The approach and landing procedure calls for a course to be flown away from the runway, passing the transmitter, "outbound station passage", travel about thirty seconds away from the station, maintaining a designated safe altitude, complete a course reversing maneuver within ten miles, then return to the transmitter. As the transmitter is crossed, the needle flips from its point toward the nose of the aircraft to point toward the tail of the aircraft. That is simply called "inbound station passage". Now, as the course to the runway is held, corrected for wind drift, the aircraft is descended to the minimum altitude allowed for the procedure where, after a stated amount of time, usually less than two minutes, the pilot who is not flying should see the runway. If the runway is not sighted, the pilot starts a climb back to a designated safe altitude and either proceeds to the predetermined alternate airport or tries another approach. It is all very safe and successful. All approaches are conducted in this same basic manner with various guidance systems and transmitters.

One night, I drove to Boston, checked my message box, and proceeded to the Crew Scheduling Department to report in. I was told that a new pilot was riding with my captain for initial checkride and that I could go home after he reported. I waited for the captain and the new pilot to arrive, and talked to them for a short time, then I caught the bus back to the parking lot and began the one-hour drive home in the rain and fog.

Before I arrived home however, catastrophe struck. After the outbound portion of the approach and before inbound station passage, the aircraft descended through the "inbound station passage" altitude striking trees and plowing into the ground. The captain and the first officer were killed instantly along with some passengers, but many passengers were saved by the heroic actions of the only flight attendant on board. Although severely injured, she directed the surviving passengers out of the elevated rear passenger door before she jumped to the ground. No one knows if, but many believe that, a premature "station passage" indication may have been the cause.

In July 1973, I had been flying my all time favorite aircraft, the McDonnell Douglas, DC-9 for six years. When I arrived at the crew lounge one foggy morning, I met my captain, who was going on vacation at the end of the day, and another captain friend. We decided that, although we had round trips to different destinations, we would arrive back in Boston about three hours later, and would have time to meet for a leisurely brunch before our next flights.

My trip proceeded to Portland, Maine while the other went to Burlington, Vermont. Upon arriving in the Boston area on our return trip, my aircraft was directed outbound, on the west side of the inbound approach course, under radar guidance. I could hear the other flight being guided behind second in line, behind me. I completed the inbound course interception under radar guidance, took over my own navigation and landed in the heavy fog, allowing the aircraft to roll to the far end of the runway. We entered taxiway "November", traveling in the opposite direction and alongside the landing runway. The fog was thick but there was good visibility when below 100 feet. I watched the next aircraft in line land on the runway that we had used. I could not contact "ground control" because of a continuous sound on their frequency and, because all other runways were closed, we continued to our assigned concourse C, gate 26.

I went inside to await my breakfast appointment and decided to say "hello" to the Chief Pilot's secretary. I opened the door and found her in tears. I asked her the reason and she said "one of our airplanes is lost". I asked which flight and she answered that it was flight 623. Taking that as meaning lost radio contact, I assured her that I was Flight 623 and that we lost radio contact with ground control but we were all safely at the gate. Just then, the Chief Pilot came into the room and said, "They think it's in the bay!"

I immediately sensed that they were talking about another flight and were using my flight number. I raced to the telephone to call my wife but the public phones had already been disconnected and the Massachusetts State Police were guarding the doors. I ran to crew Scheduling and my daughter was already on the phone asking about my flight. They told her that I was standing there and hung up. I proceeded to tell the Chief Pilot the story of the lost radio contact, but he finally told me that it was my friend's Flight 723. We later found that all passengers (except one soldier) and all six crewmembers were fatally injured. The aircraft had hit the water, "skipped" over the seawall and landed on the runway inverted.

The captain with whom I had been flying went on vacation and I was deposed to a hotel, offered liquor and asked to tell the New York lawyers what happened and what I would have done. I told them that I didn't drink, and also that I had to fly the next day, but that didn't stop the offers. I finally told them that I couldn't say what I would have done because I didn't know how the captain felt. They didn't understand that. I explained that many things affect your thinking process, and that I would refuse to give my opinion as to what happened on flight 723. Next morning, after that late night duty, I stood in the door of the cockpit welcoming the lawyers on board, and I made a special effort to look each one of them "smack in the eye". Most of them looked down at the floor after seeing that I was flying them home to New York.

Ironically, that was probably the only time in my airline career that my wife Marie had known the number of the flight that I was flying, Flight 623. Neither of us knows why she knew this particular one. She had taken my son to the Lawrence airport that morning for a flight lesson, his first solo, and one of my old acquaintances asked her if she had heard about the flight that had crashed in Boston with only one survivor. The news had stated that it was Flight 623. She couldn't call Crew Scheduling but our daughter, who worked for the telephone company, asked her supervisor's help in getting a call through, which she did. That was the call that I mentioned previously. The lone survivor, the soldier, died shortly thereafter.

Sea Fog

Fog forms when certain meteorological conditions are met. Of course, I know this from teaching meteorology for the Army, the Air Force and the airlines, and also from having to coordinate with my weather departments to predict just when and where fog may form and how it would affect changes in planning and executing my flight operations. It changes so quickly locally, that the captain must go it alone most times in his decisions, relying completely on his training and experience.

After I retired from the aviation profession, I still used my computer to forecast weather for myself, (I don't trust anyone else), for private flying and boating, especially boating in the ocean. No one is one hundred percent accurate on sea-fog forecasts.

Once, my brother in law and I decided we would drive my small aluminum fishing boat seven miles down the beach, from the mouth of the Merrimack river to the end of the peninsula of Plum Island, to fish for flounder. The little boat had a small engine, a depth-finder, and two cans of fuel. The forecast called for very light winds, warm weather, and good visibility; a perfect day. We began on our trip at first light.

After arriving at the fishing grounds, I became uneasy. Something didn't feel right but I couldn't determine just what was wrong. After only a few minutes of unproductive fishing, I heard a hissing noise. I looked seaward and saw a "curtain" coming toward us. At first I thought I was having familiar sea-vision problems where the color of the water blends with the color of the sky, but then I heard the soft hissing sound of a shower in the water, and knew immediately that we were in deep trouble. Fog trouble!

The fog curtain covered us immediately and totally. We could not even see each other in a fourteen foot boat. We pulled the lines in and began running a compass heading along the beach toward the river channel. But how was I to find the entrance? This river is the seventh most dangerous river entrance in the world, even if I find it.

I told Dave my plan. I would run the approximate number of minutes we had spent to get to our fishing spot, on the opposite compass heading, and then look for the channel, which is marked by a bell buoy. Then, we would try our luck. If we couldn't find the channel we would run the boat slowly toward the beach until it hit the sandy bottom and desert it.

I worried about the "roller" waves at the river entrance, which can become huge for ships, and especially for a little boat with eighteen-inch sides. A tuna fisherman once told me that, if I ever got caught in a surprise sea fog and wanted to find the channel entrance buoy, which is located at the end of the southernmost of the two rock jetties, that I should find the 30-foot depth and follow it. In "mean low tide", the buoy sits in thirty feet of water. In higher tides, it would be in deeper water but would be to seaward, which would be on my right.

While running along our course, I changed to a full tank of fuel. The original tank still had plenty of fuel but I, psychologically, wanted the fuller tank. Then after the estimated time had passed, I decided to turn toward the beach, as we hadn't heard the buoy. I slowed and asked Dave to sit in the front of the boat to look for the beach. Finally we both spotted a white object at the same time. "What is that Dave?" I asked, as I reversed the engine. "It's a woman!" Dave yelled. "Ask her where the Merrimack River jetties are", I said. The lady answered, "I don't know, I am from New Jersey!" I had to laugh at such luck while I backed away. I didn't want to abandon my boat and turned to try a little longer.

After a while, without finding the buoy, I tried for shore again hoping we would see some recognizable object. A surfer appeared from the fog at the same time that we spotted a large rock, with green grass and a small tree growing on top, which to this day, I cannot find again. The surfer was a young man about seventeen. Dave asked him the location of the jetties and he said, "Down that way!" pointing to where we had come from. I decided to try my luck once more, before deserting the boat. I don't know why I was trying to save a boat when it was insured, but I guess that's human nature and pride mixed together.

As I turned, a wave "broad-sided" the little boat. I saw it coming and had prepared for it by piercing it on a forty-five degree angle, but it still soaked us. However, the boat had no water inside and I proceeded on my southerly heading. I would hold a heading so that, if the depth sensor indicated less than thirty feet, I would turn seaward, or if more than thirty feet, I would turn toward shore. Then, I heard it!

Just slightly above the deafening roar of an incoming sea meeting an outgoing river, I heard the bell. Just as suddenly, I saw the bell buoy and immediately turned westward to follow the river. I soon realized that I was south of the south jetty. I immediately reversed course, found the bell again and turned north for what seemed a long time, but was probably only a few minutes, then turned west again. Once I knew I had entered the mouth of the Merrimac, I turned more toward the northerly heading to find the north jetty, seeking protection from the roller waves that were entering the river mouth.

Soon, we found a buoy, called "the toothpick", a familiar green buoy with the number 7 clearly painted on its side. I turned to a 337 degree heading, from habit formed by thirty years of sailing this river, and within a few minutes, popped out of the dense fog into perfectly clear weather. Boats were everywhere. These were boats that had been caught like us, in this unforecast sea fog, but they had navigation systems to use to come out of the fog...

I gave that boat, the engine, depth finder and all its equipment to Dave for use in the inner lakes. After that, no matter what the forecaster said, I only went to sea in my ocean-going motorsailer with satellite navigation, radio, radar and an automatic pilot. I could and did, travel great distances through dense fog, completely relaxed and safe.

I will never forget the helpless feeling of seeing that curtain of fog close in, catching me without those aids. I still look for that rock and sometimes wonder if it was some sort of illusion. Dave and I both saw it and discussed its existence (or rather, non-existence) many times. I've returned to the point, and always try unsuccessfully, to find the reason that we each saw a non-existing object. I'll never understand the puzzle of this rock in the fog with the evergreen on top and the surfer. Could it have been an illusion caused by stress? Would an illusion have happened to two people at the same instant? I don't think so, but strange things do happen in the sea, especially in a foggy sea!

I have a good friend at the American Yacht Club named Gregg. A few years ago, some club members were gathered in the clubhouse to watch a heavy storm. In front of the clubhouse, a line of floating docks was bobbing up and down in the raging Merrimack River. Gregg went to the docks to see if he could see his new sailboat through the heavy fog. He had sold his previous boat, and the person who had purchased her had her moored about a half mile away, toward the mouth of the river.

Gregg was doing a balancing act as the docks rode the choppy waters. He couldn't see his new boat but, to his amazement, the bow of another boat appeared, approaching the docks out of the fog with a dock line already in place, and hanging from the bow. He took the line and pulled the bow closer to where he could tie it to the chocks, all the while wondering just who would be out in a boat in this storm, and how they could navigate safely through the 100 boat mooring field during a storm. By now, others came to lend a hand and Gregg went aboard to assist the captain. But he found no captain; no one was aboard the boat. Furthermore, now that Gregg looked at the boat, he found that it was the same one that he had sold before purchasing his new one.

After the storm was over, he found that the boat had been moored downriver with two mooring lines. It had broken both lines in the storm, and had traveled through the complete mooring field, evidently without hitting any other boat, and had found its way to the dock where its previous owner, Gregg, was standing.

I love sea stories, especially true stories such as this. It seems that fog always contributes to these stories. Fog reflects light at different angles and differing light shades and is usually connected to movement and appearances where spooky, non-existing things suddenly appear. But this time, it was real!

+++

To The Readers;
This is the story of my last trip on my beloved sailboat, "NICKELODEAN". Although I have changed the name of her new homeport, and owner, the remainder of this story is factual.

The poetry contained herein, {within brackets}, is my copyrighted poetry from the books; {"REVERIE" A Kaleidoscope of the Prose and Poetry in My Life-2004}, or {"POT O'GOLD" Prose, Poetry and A Tale O'thu Sea-2005}, which may be ordered from the publisher, Publish America at; www.PublishAmerica.com or Barnesandnoble.com or from any major bookseller.

+++

Goodbye Nickelodean

{My ship digs her bow deep down in a wave;
Her recovery leaves me all wet.
She gives credence to a thought that I hold dear; that
My life's not over yet!}

"Take the wheel Rachel, please!" "Sure thing Grandpa!" With that, I went below where Bill was standing in ankle deep water. "What is that?" I asked. He looked at me with a worried look in his eyes, "Do you want to call the Coast Guard now or head directly to shore?" he asked. I, along with Bill, an airline captain, Bob, a Naval Academy graduate, and Billy, my son-in-law and computer expert, my two granddaughters, Roxanne the oldest, and Rachel, had left the American Yacht Club in Newburyport, Massachusetts at the precisely scheduled 3PM. It was to be our last sail on my boat, Nickelodean, a Lancer "Powersailor" and we had only been underway for an hour or so. We were delivering the boat to her new owner, a non-trusting, disagreeable man in his mid forties with little experience in deep water sailing or sailboats. He and I had disagreed on everything from the history records of the boat to the gratis delivery of the boat to Newport.

"Where is the water coming from?" "I don't know!" Bill answered and continued his concern, "I believe it could be from the holding tank." "No way, Bill!" I quipped. "The holding tank cannot leak more than it holds and there's a lot of water here. The sea-cocks can't normally leak because they are well above the waterline, but Rachel is carrying about fifteen degrees of heel and the port side lines are lower." With that I grabbed the vise-grips and hurriedly scrambled up the ladder, sliding along the empty cockpit bench seat to the port lazaret and I was under the cockpit floor in a flash. There was the culprit in full view. There was a clear plastic sump-pump hose running from the center of the boat over to and alongside the boat's hull, just about level with the waterline, to the overboard exit point in the transom. It had been split by pressure from someone's shoe (probably mine) while working on the batteries, the water heater, or fuel or oil tanks.

A quick squeeze and the vise-grips locked on, stopping the flow of the Atlantic, backward to the sump. I returned to where Bill had exposed the sump to find a smile and a receding water level. The second pump, which had been overcome, immediately emptied the floors of all standing water.

We decided to keep watch for a recurrence and I briefed the crew on what had happened. Soon, all Nickelodean's passengers were settled into their niche and I began re-trimming the sails to the following "formula" that I had worked out to keep my sequence routine.

STD HH
S-Sails set initially
T-Traveler adjusted for even leading edge chord
D-Draft adjusted for 10 to 12 inch depth
H-Heel within limits of 12 to 18 degrees
H-Helm about 8 degrees or less

I initially run this formula over about three times in succession, and then repeat it after a course change, or a change in the wind direction or velocity.

Rachel had the course set to 135 degrees when I relieved her and pushed the button to turn the auto-pilot on. The initialization had begun in a rapid series of hums but soon started to quiet, until no sound was made.

{Oh God; my philosophical bent lies dormant 'till I meet the sea.
Her aura sets my heart a' beat and now my trip's begun,
I am at rest.}

Nickelodean began to sing her usual low-pitched hum, which told me that her cruising speed had been attained, and I eased the mainsheet just enough to allow the tell-tales to rest in their cruising position, just aft of the vertical. I looked at Rachel and Roxanne and we shared a smile at the speed she was holding. The thrill of a perfectly trimmed boat was running through our veins. We were flying smoothly at the wonderful speed of 7 1/2 knots. Our song was being sung through Nickelodean's rigging lace. The wind-song matched the hum of her cruise sound beautifully, making heavenly sounds, known to all sailors.

{Tack to windward, run to lee
and take me Nickelodean with thee.
To where? I do not know, nor care,
as long as I'm with you.}

We were holding a great starb'd tack, directly southeast with a beautiful high-pressure area located just southeast of New Jersey, giving us a west-southwesterly wind. If I had the power to order a wind, this was what I would have requested. The velocity of 25 knots however, was slightly more than I would have asked for, placing four, and occasionally five-foot waves before us, but I won't argue with it. I expected some moderate wave activity anyway as we passed Cape Ann's influence. But Nickelodean's five foot bow handled them beautifully. We dined on Italian grinders and Rachel and Roxanne took a much needed break. They had spent much of the afternoon alternating turns at the helm, moving Nickelodean past Cape Ann into open water.

As darkness settled in, we could see the lights and the taller buildings of Boston and we were under the approach pattern to the west runway at Logan Airport about twenty miles away. The aircraft overhead were slowed to about 210 knots, in trail and leaving 6,000 feet on their initial approach to runway 27. For a few minutes, we listened to the flight crew/controller conversations on the ship's radio. Because I was engaged in that profession for many years, I could tell my crew what duties were being performed and what the pilot/controller conversations were about, all along their path to touchdown.

Before I took the helm we had prepared the boat for night running. Radar was tuned, crew's watches had already been assigned and now reviewed. Emergency equipment was checked and discussed, along with its location, lights were turned on, and lanterns and spotlights checked. The route was discussed and, as we held a course for Provincetown, I re-trimmed the sails at least twice, dressed the line ends, cleared the decks and stowed all unneeded equipment as the boat quieted and nighttime fell.

{I set my sails, as all sailors have done,
to capture Heaven's breeze.
The songs sung through my riggings lace
sets my old heart at ease.}

A high powered spotlight is always kept by the helmsman to light up the sails whenever another boat or ship approaches. I must admit that I used that spotlight a few times to look at the waves that we were encountering. They were smaller as, with darkness, the wind had relaxed to about 12 to 15 knots. Now, as the "high" moved eastward, winds and waves had shifted to a more southerly direction and about as close to the bow as the boat could handle. I disengaged the auto-pilot and changed course to port, to keep a decent speed. But I had to return to my desired course quickly, if and when I could, or lose my target, which was to fall off to the east side of the point of course change. Nickelodean was now being slapped on the starb'd side by the cross-waves and she rocked with each one. The blackness of a darkened sea always unnerves me. It reminded me of the horses on the farm where I grew up.

They were gentle and sweet animals most times but, if you considered their sheer strength, it could make you think of their capabilities.

{Creator of earth, of Heaven and space,
please grant my wishes tonight.
Bless my small ship, keep her to course,
and make the ocean quiet.}

Laughter wafted up from below decks as I watched the moonlight glisten in the choppy waters of the open ocean. I picked up the Provincetown light just starb'd of Nickelodean's bow, and the course of 135 degrees was perfect! As soon as I picked up the second Provincetown light, my plans were to keep both lights aligned until about five miles away and then turn south south-westerly into Cape Cod Bay toward Sagamore Bridge and the channel. I had to be careful not to fall asleep while admiring the beauty of the stars. I could have reached out in the darkness and touched the moon.

After the meal and refreshing cup of hot coffee, I could recognize all the voices except Rachel. I didn't hear Rachel! She must have fallen asleep. She had been on helm duty for quiet a while. My reverie was interrupted when her father, Billy came on deck to tell me that she didn't feel well. I immediately brought her up with me in the wind, but it was too late. She was seasick and terribly embarrassed about it. Of course I told her the old adage, "Show me a sailor who says he doesn't get seasick and I'll show you a liar!" But it didn't help. I checked our speed and found that we were being slowed to 4 knots by the shifting winds and waves but still would arrive at the channel at exactly the planned 7AM. Rachel rested in the cockpit bench with a blanket and pillow. Upon arriving at the five mile point northwest, from the first Provincetown light, I set a tight port tack, southwest via radar, for the Sagamore Bridge. At break of day, we visually verified the bridge. The wind had settled as expected, to almost southerly as the "high" had drifted further east and further out to sea. We were now on the outside, or trailing edge, of the clockwise flow of air.

At 7AM, Billy dropped the mainsail into the lazy-jack, furled the headsail and I started the 150 horsepower engine. I pushed the throttles forward until the boat was traveling at a smooth speed. I had stayed at the helm all night. The crew was up early, if they had slept at all and Rachel seemed to feel much better. I reported our "on-schedule" progress to the boat-yard. They asked me to call them when we were half an hour from the docks. I figured on slowing to an average of 6 knots into the heavy traffic channel, close-in, so three miles away I would call. We still had a full day of sailing ahead of us first, but I like to communicate. We had cereal and coffee and cookies for breakfast and motored through the channel.

At 8AM we left Bourne abeam Monument Beach, and still under power. Because of heavy traffic, we stayed under power until 10AM, when abeam and directly southeast of New Bedford, Massachusetts. Luck was with us. In the cool sea breeze, Rachel was feeling better. We decided to raise the sails again for a port tack. According to the Airport Traffic Information Service (ATIS) at New Bedford Airport, the wind was south-southeast at 12 knots. "Still perfect!"

With the winds from the south-southeast, we settled in for a rather quiet 6-hour sail on Long Island Sound. Someone finally brought up the fact that this was our last sail on Nickelodean and we shared memories of some of the great trips we had had. We all agreed that they were all fun, whether we made-schedule or not.

At 4PM, I called at "three miles/30 minutes out" and was soon met by a powerboat that pulled alongside, identified themselves, and asked for the keys to my car. I had delivered my car to the boatyard two days before. Apparently, when I was told where to park and lock my car, the attendant had forgotten that a boat, which was stored in back of the car, needed to be moved. They took my keys with them and left us. When we approached the docks, we were asked to delay for twenty minutes. Usually "holding patterns" are reserved for airplanes but I seem to hold more in boats. Eventually, we were invited to continue to our assigned dock, where the new owner met us.

We cleared Nickelodean of all our possessions and I turned the keys over without much ado. I showed and told him of the broken sump hose and removed my vise-grips to show him that it would not leak except when heeled on a starb'd tack. I explained again, how anyone can inadvertently step on the hose and that a metal pipeline cover should be installed there. He acknowledged it and ordered the yardmaster to replace the plastic pipe with no cover. It was done immediately. After he looked the boat over, he started the engine and asked people aboard, who accompanied him, and shortly Nickelodean obeyed her new master's command and backed away from the dock for the first time ever without my being on board. It was a sad time. I felt sick in my stomach. I would sorely miss her.

We walked to the car, heads down, and in absolute silence, with the only sound, the crunch of crushed seashells under our feet. We would all miss her! I thought, "If I were younger I would never have let her go." I took a last look. I missed her already. I felt like a traitor handing her over to someone whom I disliked. Why wouldn't she be fine? He had a lot of money invested in her.

About two weeks later, the new owner notified me by e-mail that Nickelodean had sunk on her very first voyage under sail. He had stepped on the pipe and cracked it while checking the batteries. He was sailing her alone and did not see the water entering until it was too late. The Coast Guard rescued him and the insurance company had salvaged Nickelodean. He was buying another boat. He can't buy a better boat in her class. Not in my opinion anyway. I wished her well. I did not wish him well.

Two years have passed and now I know why others have told me that a person can become attached to a material object such as a boat. I now believe them. She didn't deserve her fate, and it was my fault for selling her to someone that I didn't like as a sailor. She was a member of this family.

Remembering all the great times we had with Nickelodean, I know that I will always miss her. Goodbye old friend!

Skyhawks and Mountains

It had been about twenty years since I had flown light aircraft. When I worked for the Air Force, I belonged to an aero club that had started with a Piper Cub and had graduated to a Cessna 140, a Cessna 150, and finally, a Cessna 172 (Skyhawk). The first Skyhawk had been totally destroyed in an accident but we had bought another. Later, the aircraft that I was flying for the airlines totally occupied my thoughts, and soon I just forgot about smaller craft.

When I was 53 years of age, I was medically grounded for the second time, and I retired from the airline because of Meniere's disease, which involves a change of the structure of the inner ear. I didn't believe that I could regain my medical certification to operate aircraft. However, there are three classes of medical certificates. To simply fly aircraft solely for pleasure, you need to pass a Third Class Medical examination and possess a Private Pilot Certificate. To carry passengers for hire, you must pass a Second Class Medical examination and possess a Commercial Certificate, and to fly as a captain of passenger transport aircraft, the requirements are to pass a First Class Medical examination (renewable every six months), and possess an Airline Transport Pilots Certificate (ATP). This is the highest certificate attainable in aviation.

I decided to ask the FAA Chief Flight Surgeon for a Third Class Medical Certificate and after many months of testing, re-testing, Regional Flight Surgeon's examinations and opinions, my request was granted. Now, I wished to rent an aircraft and spend time with an FAA Flight Instructor until I felt safe to fly whatever aircraft I wished. I went to a local airport and walked in to the desk. I introduced myself to the clerk and said, "I am a retired airline captain, with an Airline Transport Pilot Certificate and approximately 25,000 hours flying time, and I would like a price for being checked out on a Skyhawk. She answered that I would need ten hours of aircraft rental time with an instructor, at a cost of one thousand dollars. Actually, I knew that I was not required to have any training at all. I told her that I would check other places and let her know.

I noticed a man standing close-by, reading a flight manual, and assumed that he was a pilot. I walked outside and, when I was seated in my car, I noticed a sign over the door that read, "Introductory Offer, solo a Skyhawk, six hours flying time with an instructor, three hours ground school, and a log book. Only $350" I went back inside and said to Evelyn, "I have never flown an aircraft. I'll take the offer on the sign." She accepted my fee and signed me up, then introduced me to the fellow I had noticed, my instructor Bud Delong.

The aircraft flight characteristics and its numbers returned to me quickly, since I had had over 200 hours in a Cessna Skyhawk many years before. The only trouble was that, when landing, because the aircraft I had flown for the last twenty years was about seven times as long, I flared much too high above the ground. After the instructor noisily and nervously pointed that out, I was fine.

We had a lot of fun because I was at home in the aircraft quickly and we had contests as to who could make the smoothest landings and/ or take off in the shortest distance.

I was released to "solo" within an hour but I hate being alone in an airplane and we often flew together. One cold Sunday morning in December, I called Bud at home and said, "Have you had breakfast?" After finding out that he hadn't, I asked if he would meet me at the airport where we could ride to Berlin, New Hampshire for breakfast. We lived south of the White Mountains and Berlin was on the north side, giving us some nice views. After our planned breakfast, we would proceed easterly to the seashore, checking out Lake Sabago, Maine on the way, and then fly over water, following the coastline south to The Isles of Shoals before turning westbound toward home.

Soon, we were in level flight at 6,500 feet above sea level, in the smoothest air I have ever flown in. It was so smooth that I removed my headset and laid it on one side of the instrument panel and soon the aircraft started banking (leaning), and turning in that direction. I then placed the headset on the opposite side of the aircraft and soon, the Skyhawk was turning in that direction. I flew a course that would place us about a mile east of the Mt. Washington peak which is 6,288 feet above sea level. It was covered with snow, as was all the terrain around us. Bud remarked that the engine was running unusually smooth in the cold air, (approximately zero degrees Fahrenheit).

At almost that precise moment, which also was the moment that we were discussing the beauty of Mt. Washington's peak in front of us, the engine stopped. I immediately followed the emergency checklist for engine failure by checking the magnetos (ignition), the fuel/air mixture, increasing the temperature of the fuel, then checking the fuel tank selector to both wing tanks. I attempted to re-start the engine to no avail. I checked the aircraft in its optimum glide speed of 85 miles per hour and remembered my formula. I remembered that this aircraft will glide 10 miles from 6,000 feet. I needed no interpolation as I was already at 6,000 feet. We had precious few choices as to where we could land in the National Forest. The highways are mostly covered by a canopy of tree branches.

.

I asked Bud to look for a clearing in the woods, perhaps made by a bulldozer, as though someone had began the first clearing for a runway. I had seen it before, as I had flown along this area, and it was on his side of the cockpit. He answered that he saw the clearing but couldn't make out just what it was. I told him that we had no other options and, in trying to keep from making too many turns with the resultant altitude loss, asked him to set up a flight path to that strip, whatever it was, and I would declare an emergency. I selected 121.5 megahertz on the VHF radio and called, "Mayday, Mayday, Mayday", I continued, "Cessna 18 Tango, Cessna Skyhawk, with an engine failure 15 miles south-southeast of Mt. Washington, squawking 7700, (emergency transponder signal code), leaving 5,400 feet, attempting emergency landing in clearing to my south. White and red aircraft based Manchester, New Hampshire. Two souls-on-board, over". It occurred to me that in all my years of flying, this was my first real emergency.

I was answered immediately by "Portland Radio, Go ahead Cessna 18 Tango". Just then another voice came in from a Canadair jet, whose vapor trail I could see directly and high above us, starting a circle. The pilot said that he had heard me and would remain overhead, relaying my information, in case the mountains interfered with my communications with Portland Radio, located at sea level on the shoreline of the Atlantic. I thanked him and acknowledged Portland Radio. Now, all we had to do was land, with no power, on whatever this "strip" contained, and hope it wouldn't destroy the aircraft and perhaps, us.

I continuously worked with the engine to attempt to get it started and it would occasionally start and run for a few seconds, not enough however to depend on, but perhaps a few lifesaving feet of propulsion would come in handy. It never hurts!

Bud had aligned the aircraft with the "strip" by the time I had all this completed but, because I was the senior pilot and this was my aircraft, I said, "Are you o.k. with this, or do you want me to take it?" He said he felt fine but didn't know what type of surface we were landing on. I told him that I would follow him through and we flared to land. The aircraft touched down and we expected the landing gear to perhaps, collapse but we rolled bumpily, albeit smoother than expected. We lifted the left wing as an object appeared, and as the wing rose up slightly, a sign zipped under that read, "No Snowmobiles".I had to laugh as we slowed to a stop, half from relief and half about the sign.

The propeller had been "wind-milling" during our descent but now I noticed that it was turning by itself with no wind to help it. The engine had started again on its own as we touched down on the bumpy, but smoother than trees, river-rock "runway". I thanked the Canadair Jet pilot, profusely I think, and he sped away, towards Canada.

We got out of the aircraft, which now had an odor with which I was familiar with but couldn't recall for a while. Then, I remembered when I worked with flight simulators where electronic switches were insulated with a material called "phenolic board". I didn't know why but the aircraft smelled strongly of this material. We walked to find a telephone. After a short time, we came upon a group of houses but no one was at home. Then, two men in an oil delivery truck came along and we flagged them down. Bud volunteered to go with them to find a phone and call FAA. I walked back to the aircraft.

As I approached our aircraft, another aircraft was aligned with our newly commissioned runway and, as I pointed to the sign, he landed as far as he could from it. He had greatly oversized tires on the aircraft for snow and rough terrain landings. Two men got out with the first "bag-phone" I had ever seen, placed it on the tail surface of my aircraft and asked, "Is there anyone you would like to call?" Of course, I called Marie and reported that we were o.k., and then I called our home airport, so they wouldn't start a search for us. But just as I thanked my rescuer for the phone, it rang. He answered and said "It's for you!" Baffled, I answered and an FAA Inspector asked if I was O.K.. I answered affirmatively. Then he asked about the problem with the engine. I explained, and he said, "stay with the airplane, we'll be there shortly by helicopter." I asked the rescue aircraft pilot if we could get a ride with him as I noticed that Bud had returned. The pilot said, "Anytime!" I told the FAA Inspector that he could find the aircraft right where it was and that we were going to the nearest restaurant to eat and then go home. With that, we boarded the rescue aircraft and took off to begin our trip home.

The rescue pilot told us that he had been in his office when he heard my "mayday" on his radio monitor, heard the exact GPS position, thought that we were in real trouble, and had brought his mechanic to search for us. He hadn't thought of landing on this rocky strip, but after seeing that we had landed on it, he reasoned that, with his large balloon tires, he should be able to use it also. We expressed our sincere thanks to them as they brought us to

Laconia, New Hampshire. I tried to pay them for their expenses, but they refused to take the money.

We talked for a while and asked how we might be able to get to Manchester, where our cars were parked. They said that they had a car for their summer guests that we could take, free of charge, and could leave it at the Manchester airport and they would pick it up later. We left with a relatively new Pontiac sedan and soon realized that we hadn't had anything to eat all day. We stopped at the Tilton Diner near the Interstate and had a meal. I can't remember if it was breakfast, lunch or dinner or all three, but we ate. When we walked back to the car, I saw a great amount of green fluid under it. Anti-freeze had somehow been discharged from the engine radiator or block. I called the owner who said that he would pick it up, and also send someone to drive us to our destination. We returned to the diner for coffee and pie. The waitress, seeing our return, asked Bud what we were doing. Bud answered that, "We were flying to breakfast, lost our engine and had to do an emergency landing on rocks, near Mount Washington. When we were rescued, we left our airplane where it landed and we were flown to Laconia. Then the cooling system in the new car we had borrowed burst and we decided to have a piece of pie and coffee before a chauffeured car comes to pick us up and drive us home!" The waitress roared with laughter and said, "You are so funny!"

Later, it was discovered that the engine of the Cessna had been removed for maintenance, two years prior to our flight. When it was re-installed, the "grounding strap" was inadvertently left off. The engine was being grounded through the ignition wire cover. After two years, the cover had started to deteriorate and failed to allow the ignition to ground properly. We were lucky to find a place to land safely.

I fell in love with a small, "Geronimo" Apache, A Piper Aircraft Twin-engined airplane that was for sale, and in which I wanted to be checked-out. It had been modified with better (more powerful) engines than the original aircraft, and could carry four adults, with luggage, comfortably. I soon was cleared to fly it solo, and I took my daughter and son-in-law for a ride to see the ski slopes and the ocean. We landed in Portland, Maine for fuel and continued sight-seeing for a while before returning to Lawrence, Massachusetts, where the aircraft was based. I loved the safety of two engines and the roomy interior.

I thought about it for a long while and talked it over with Marie, and we decided to purchase it. I drove to the airport and, as I parked, I watched it lift off the runway for another flight. I went inside and asked the airport operator what time the Gerinomo was scheduled to be back, and he said, "It just took off for Texas. It has been sold. It was a sad ride home.

Pilot Humor

I had the absolute pleasure of flying often with a Captain Charlie Jacobsen. We both knew our jobs well and found humor in the same things, and we laughed from the time we reported for work until we arrived back home, sometimes four days later. Immediately after the merger of Northeast and Delta Airlines, the North and the South, I, being a Rebel, was attempting the additional job of teaching Charlie, the Yankee, the "Southern" language. We had flown the "Deep South" routes for nearly a month, when Charlie felt confident enough to try to hold an audience with an unsuspecting southern Air Traffic Controller, using the local tongue. I was flying the aircraft, it was a beautiful night and we had the runways in sight. Charlie began to show off his newly acquired verbal skills by using the aircraft's communication radio.

"Whut's thu name o' that swamp down 'ere?" he asked. "'At ain't no swamp, 'at's Cross Lake," the controller replied while watching our blip on radar. Charlie felt good about this exchange and said, "I bet tere's a lotta good fishin' in 'ere too, ain't tey?" "Yea! Ye oughtta come on down sometimes and we'll go catch us some," retorted the controller. Charlie was ecstatic! He asked me how he was doing, obviously bragging. "Real good," I said. "I would think you lived down the street from the controller, Charlie!" He just couldn't leave it alone and said, "I bet tere's uh lotta 'watermouths' in 'ere too, ain't tey?" The controller snapped back, "Ah you from Baustin, Suh?" I wouldn't tell Charlie for hours what he did wrong. Finally, I told him there's no such snake as a watermouth.

Charlie and I had a midwinter trip to our northernmost stop in the United States, the frozen tundra of Presque Isle, Maine. We had a full ship with not one empty seat.

Charlie was flying the airplane and on arrival, commanded me to lower the landing gear. I placed the lever in the down position and the indicator lights flashed back green, green and amber! "Whoops, recycle!" I lifted the lever, and when the lights extinguished, placed the lever back to the down position. Green, green and amber! "It's probably frozen slush interfering with the micro-switch. Better go look," Charlie said.

Of course, we flew the airplane while we were in shirtsleeves, and sometimes with ties loosened. When going into an area where passengers could see us, we dressed "class- A". So I got fully dressed with my double-breasted jacket with gold braid, gold buttons and gold stripes, tie straight and hat on, complete with "gold scrambled eggs" covering the visor. Now I proceeded to a position half way through the cabin, to a point that is over the landing gear inspection point.

Here, while trying to act nonchalantly, I kneeled down on my knees, pulled the carpet away from the viewer, removed the cover plate, and pulled the periscope, that is provided for looking at the landing gear, up and out of its container. I turned it to bring the right landing gear mechanism into focus, and then placed my eye on the periscope. Frigid air being forced up and around the tube caused my eye to stream tears as if someone had poured water in it. The gear was locked down! I swung the viewer to the left gear and repeated the procedure. Now both eyes were streaming tears. While still on my knees, I noticed a lady sitting beside my left shoulder, also in tears and saying her Rosary. While still on my knees, with tears running down my face, and replacing the removed cover and carpet, I tried to explain to her, in a convincing way, that we were having a safe flight.

People who grew up in Maine have a wonderful, slow accent, which sometimes, sounds very comical. For example, "A-yuh" means the same as "yeah" in other parts of the country and "Ah-yul" means "I'll, or "I will". One of the captains that I most liked to fly with, when I was a first officer, was a man named Hugh Murray. He was from northern New Hampshire, but his thinking, his speech, and his thoughts were definitely from Maine. One morning, we started our flight schedule from Bangor, Maine in an airplane that had been parked outside all night, in extremely cold temperatures, while loaded with fuel and cargo, and we were to start our day with a very short, ten minute trip to Portland, Maine.

The tires were constructed of nylon and had frozen to their "flat-on-the-bottom" position during their long cold exposure. With the passengers aboard and Hilda, an especially buxom flight attendant from Germany, serving the front of the cabin, we started to taxi. The tires were so out of shape that we had to stop a few times to regain our composure from the rather severe shaking of the fuselage when the flat side of the tires hit the pavement. Soon however, we started our take-off roll and with the increasing speed the vibration was tremendous. I yelled my required "call-outs" at the top of my voice, "Engine power checked, V-1, Rotate, V-2" and as Hugh pulled the Boeings nose into the air the shaking continued. However, the landing gear slowed their rotation soon, and when retracted, a "snubber-brake" stopped the tires from rotating and the flight smoothed out. Usually, the heat generated from the friction of takeoff, allows the flat spots to round out, but not that day. They were too cold to round out. When we landed at Portland and the wheels started rolling again, the aircraft shook violently. Soon, we parked on the ramp and a portable, motorized set of stairs with a platform on top was driven to the aircraft door.

After the passengers left, Hugh and I dressed in our jackets and hats and went to the platform on our way to the restaurant for breakfast. On the platform, and as usual, we were met by our two mechanics. One was very tall and skinny with an unlighted cigarette dangling from his lips and a tool pouch hanging from his hip and the other, extremely short with the same type of tool pouch. They greeted us in their thick Maine accent, "Hello, fellas" anything wrong with the ai-uh-plane?" Hugh answered in an equally thick Maine accent, "A-yuh! The ty-yuhs ah sqa-yuh and Hilda broke her bra strap!"
Without one hint of a smile, the shorter of the two mechanics immediately started down the stairs and, looking back, said, "Ah-yul check the ty-yuhs!"

I flew, as First Officer with a wonderful fellow from the Lakes Region of New Hampshire. Captain John was born I'm sure, with a smile on his face. I don't think he had the power to remove it. He and I had a schedule together for a month that included four, four-day trips, that brought us to New Orleans every Monday night in the month. We arrived at 2:00 p.m. and left at 8:00 a.m., which gave us time to shower and rest during the heat of the afternoon, then eat at the best restaurant we could find each night before the crowds arrived. It worked beautifully and we got to Bourbon Street in time to see the best shows.

We ate some of the best food in the city and had seen all the entertainers that we wanted to see, including Pete Fountain, Al Hirt and The Preservation Hall Band. On the last trip to our hotel, we were walking past an establishment that we hadn't seen before. John mentioned that those beautiful "ladies" that we could see on their stage inside, were not ladies at all. I said, "They are ladies John! They want you to think they are men dressed as women but they are really pretty women!" "Well, let's find out!" he said. We discussed a plan then entered. The band was loud and the people noisy. I really didn't think that he would follow the plan, but I wanted to watch him "turn chicken". We sat down at a tiny table and when the "waitress" asked me for my order, I answered with a greatly lowered voice. When "she" bent over to ask me what I had said, I heard a horrible "yelp" from "her" and we briskly departed the area, blending into the crowded street and laughing as we hurriedly walked toward our hotel. All John would say was, "You're wrong!"

Jake a.k.a. Scotty

As you danged-well know by now, I love animals. This is a true story of a cat, with more than one name and more than one residence, that I know as "Jake".

Winter's wrath can be quite severe in New Hampshire. These super-cold spells last for a day or for ten days, but they are extraordinarily cold. I buy food for the animals (all of them) in our forest. Nuggets and apples for the deer, bread and dog food for the raccoons, small seeds for the small birds and sunflower seeds for the larger ones. Even coyotes eat the sunflower seeds and dog food, relieving the "food chain" stress on the other animals. The bears are asleep.

My speedboat and trailer had been lifted to rest on blocks, covered with a tarpaulin, and stored between the house and the shrub garden. The excess "tarp" hung down to the ground and the wind-blown snow had piled up to about three feet around the circumference of the whole package.

Jack Frost himself was looking for a place to hide for about two weeks. It was extremely cold, causing me to be concerned about the forest creatures. As I checked their food supply each evening, I could hear the cry of an animal that could have been a cat, (wild or domestic), or some other small animal, but I couldn't see it. The cry was almost a howl and was coming from under the tarpaulin, but when I would try to get a closer look, the animal would become silent and hide.

I continued my quest of getting closer each day with the food, and I eventually coaxed a beautiful young male cat to trust me. He had long fangs, that extended well below his lower jaw, which made him look like the drawings of a saber-tooth tiger. His coat was the color of copper with lighter stripes of gold. He must have been under that boat for a week, and was nearly frozen. I picked him up and carried him inside to a blanket in the kitchen, and fed him cat food and warm milk. Soon, after a long warm sleep, he was happily strolling about the house, getting to know the two cats, Tommy and Gerry, that Marie had rescued from "death row", and another cat, that we had named Elwood, that had also come in unannounced, however permanently, from the woods.

We had an Elwood, so "Jake" was the natural choice for a name. I would pick him up and he would close his eyes and rub my chin with the top of his head. Our German Shepherd dog, Charlie thought it was great to have these new family members. Soon, one other "calico" cat, we would name Flora, would join us. All happily remained rather indefinitely.

By Spring, all had been examined, inoculated, neutered and licensed and were living together in harmony. "Jake", however, had a habit of yelling loudly somewhat like a coyote howl. He could purr long and hard but his "meow" was more of a song.

On one particular day, a car entered our driveway and a woman and small girl came in and asked about the cat we called "Jake". The little girl called him "Scotty" and the cat went to her, and was right at home in her arms, eyes closed, purring, and rubbing her chin with the top of his head. He was her cat all right, and they drove away with our "Jake" or their "Scotty" to his home, about a half a wooded mile away. We were sad to see him leave but glad the little girl had found her pet.

Next morning I went down to the kitchen and glanced at the deck. There, howling in all his glory, was our "Jake". Happy to be home, he joined all the rest for breakfast, meowing and purring with glee. He had walked through the snowy woods to return to us. We enjoyed his company for the rest of the day because his "parents" worked. When they came home, I called to tell them that their "Scottie" was again, at our house. They picked him up and took him home.

Next day, "Jake" announced his arrival at five AM with the cry of a small mountain lion. He was back. Then, after the owners had returned to their home, I called again. This time, he saw them driving up our driveway and ran to hide. He found a great place because they could not find him. After they left, he returned to join his new family. The owners would return on their own, to look for him, but he became more and more adept at hiding. The little girl came with the parents on one occasion and was walking through our yard, which adjoins the woods, calling "Scotty". I happened to look behind a tree and "Jake" was hiding there but as they walked by, he slowly changed his position to stay exactly opposite their position, and remain hidden behind the tree. That intelligence shocked me! However, I unwittingly did something then that I would regret for a long time. I pointed out his location and they drove away with him. They told me before they left, that they would lock him up, so that he would not come back again. I constantly thought of "Jake" as I passed his street for the next four years. I still like a traitor.

However, one summer night, we were watching television and heard a strange sound. I muted the television and heard the once familiar cry of our "mountain lion". He had come to us after having been locked up in his home for four years. We were smothered with head/chin rubs and purring and the cries of joy for a while, then he began to walk around. Elwood and Tom had died but Flora and Gerry were still living with us. However, after sitting quietly by himself, for a time, "Jake", for some unknown reason, attacked Flora and Gerry. I had to call his "parents" and tell them that I couldn't have their "Scotty" come back and hurt the others.

I felt terrible as I said goodbye to an animal that had remembered us during four years of imprisonment. It was so sad to see him being taken away. He rode in back seat of the car like a gentleman, but looked back at us as he traveled down the driveway to his home again. A couple of years passed and another copper cat, with a white "bib" showed up to reside with us. We named him Tommy. Now, Tommy and Flora were our only remaining domestic animals.

But alas, nothing is forever and five full years after his last ride home; Marie opened the slider to let Tommy come inside for the night. He immediately went to her room. Next morning, she told me that she had let Tommy in, and that he had gone to her room and was told to go downstairs, which he did. However, she had found him in her closet again and, again he had now been sent downstairs. I informed her that Tommy slept beside me all night. She hurried downstairs to "Jake" and a great homecoming. "Jake" had returned after five more years. He gave us his head rubbing under our chin, purring with closed eyes, then, after a wonderful visit, wanted to go outside. We opened the sliding door and let him go. He voluntarily walked through the woods and home. Our hearts were happy and our hearts were broken, simultaneously.

I have cared for many, many pets and wild animals. On different occasions, we had two raccoons that lived for a winter in the shed and also in our house. The female later brought her cubs home to us. There is many a story to tell of bears and cubs, horses, dogs and a pair of fisher cats, but we can never forget the cat with two names. We will always remember, miss, and love our "Jake". Wouldn't you?

Book Bonus #2
Muse Season

CONTENTS

You Might Be a Farm Kid If

YOU MIGHT BE A FARM KID, IF YOU REMEMBER THESE SOUNDS

"Plink"	minnows playing in the creek.
"Toodle-oop-toodle-oodle-oop"	sound from a running stream
"Aaaaaaak- aaaaaaak"	corn leaves rubbing in a gentle summer breeze
"Chuck-chick, chuck-chick"	mule walking through gravel
"Ummmmm"	contented cow mooing in the nighttime
"Luuuck luck-luck"	contented chickens scratching in dirt
"Aaaaaak aak aak"	ducks enjoying a swim

YOU MIGHT BE A FARM KID IF YOU HAVE;

Watched piglet's birth and hear them immediately squeak and fight for feeding position.
Watched a new colt run?
Watched a calf stand for the first time?
Watched minnows swim through clumps of aromatic mint in the creek.
Rested in the shade of a swaying weeping willow in a soft summer's breeze?
Enjoyed the smell of a horse's leather harness.
Felt the bond, as an animal puts his trust in you.

A Little Acorn at Panther Springs

(A Conversation)

Hey, Mister! You're from around here, aren't you?

NO! ER YES! ER, WHO'S ASKING? WHO'S THERE?

Now don't get so excited, Boy! It's just the old oak tree that you're sitting under. Nice shade, huh?

WHY YES, I GUESS SO! WHO'S THERE?

Don't worry; I just need to talk to someone sometimes. I was just thinking that I haven't seen you around for a while, now.

I NEVER TALKED TO A TREE; I MEAN, I WAS BORN OVER THERE A WAYS, ACROSS THAT MOUNTAIN, OVER SEVENTY YEARS AGO.

I know! So why did you say "no"!

WELL, I LIVE AWAY NOW AND I USUALLY SAY I AM FROM THE PLACE WHERE I LIVE. BESIDES, NOTHING VERY IMPORTANT HAPPENED AROUND HERE; I COULDN'T WAIT TO GROW UP AND LEAVE WHEN I WAS A YOUNG MAN.

Well, now! I'll just bet that this little town could give the town you say you're from now a little competition.

WHAT DO YOU MEAN?

I have been living here beside this old spring for a few hundred years now. When I was just a sapling, I remember many meetings, held right there in that clearing, between the Creek and Cherokee Chiefs. They danced and smoked and talked about the many white men that were coming through their lands. Why, Daniel Boone, himself was only six years old, back in 1740, when he stopped by the spring for a rest and a cool drink. Said he was going hunting for bar. Ha! That's what he called a bear. He also had some story as to why they named this Panther Springs. There were panthers around here then. Yessiree! I've seen some big ones drink here. Dan'l, as folks around here called him, went on to be a great frontiersman and woodsman and in 1769, he and his friend John Findlay lead a group of men, like himself, through the Cumberland Gap into Kentucky and founded the town of Boonesboro, where he lived for a while.

SURE, SOME GREAT WOODSMEN WERE BORN HERE, BUT....

Now wait a minute, there's nothing wrong with being a great woodsman, when you live in the woods, is there? Let me tell you about another great woodsman and frontiersman born here. He was also a great politician and an even greater soldier. Right up here on the banks of the Nolichucky River, David Crockett was born in 1786, and shortly thereafter, began to show his colors as a hunter and a politician. The Creeks and Cherokees had massacred his grandfather and 12 others up East of here near the river in Rogersville in 1777. Of course, that was nine years before Davy was born. He spent many a day hunting here around the springs and river; he became known as a great orator. As a young man, he moved down to Jefferson City. He didn't learn to read and write until he was eighteen years old. Then he went on to become a Tennessee Legislator and an U.S. Congressman for six years. Did you know that?

YEAH, BUT.

Hold on, I see I need to tell you more! About ten years after Davy was born, a new kid moved into the area with his widowed mother and raised right here in Tennessee. He visited me from time to time. He lived with the Cherokee for three years and learned their language and customs. He did a stint with the Army, fighting in the Creek Indian War with Andrew Jackson then resigned to study law and became a U.S. Senator. He was also Adjutant General, then Governor of Tennessee. He was President of the Territory of Texas and presided over her independence. Then he became the U.S. Senator from his new State of Texas and finally the Governor of the Great State of Texas. You might say that he was promoted from President to Governor. He was also a General of the Army of the United States. Sam Houston still has a town named for him in his beloved Texas. I hear it's a pretty big town, too! He and Davy became good friends. He was training an army to defend the Alamo but it was too late. For 13 days, 200 brave people, along with Davy Crockett and another frontiersman, Colonel Jim Bowie, a friend from Arkansas, defended the Alamo from General Santa Anna's Army. But on the morning of the fourteenth day, all the guns were quiet. Yep! Sonny, You can be plenty proud to have been from Tennessee. Why, The

Tennessee National Guard Unit, the 278th Infantry of which, if my memory is correct, you were a member of when you left, has distinguished itself during the Korean and the Iraqi Wars. They were just welcomed home again in November 2005, by a proud and grateful County. And isn't your name carved on that monument in the Hamblen County Court yard?

IT IS!

Did you know that Calvin J. Ward from Hamblen County was awarded the Medal of Honor for single handedly wiping out an enemy machine-gun nest in France in 1918? And just one year later, in 1919 and also in France, Edward R. Talley did exactly the same thing, and was also awarded the Medal of Honor? Hamblen County was the only county in America with two Medal of Honor winners. I'm still the proudest oak in the forest, Boy! Tennessee was home of many great men. Names like York, Jefferson, Jackson and Polk were honored right here in my shade. I know I am proud that hundreds of years ago, an acorn dropped right here in this spot, made itself to home, and I have made it my home to this day. Do you hear me Son?

YES, SIR! I AM PROUD OF MY COUNTY, MY COUNTRYMEN AND MY HOME. BUT THOSE FOLKS WERE WOODSMEN AND FRONTIERSMEN AND...

I hear Ya! You're talkin' "modern" technology, aren't you, Boy?

WELL, THERE WERE NO HENRY FORDS NOR WRIGHT BROTHERS NOR...

Oh! You think not, do you? I believe you flew airplanes for a profession, didn't you?

YES SIR! I TAUGHT MILITARY KIDS HOW TO FLY AND THEN I FLEW AIRLINERS. WHY?

Because, a 21 year old farmer sat right where you are sitting on December the 4th, eighteen hundred and seventy six, nineteen years before your dad was born, and wrote to his friend, Will Turner, in South Dakota about a flying machine, an ornithopter he had designed and built. He wrote, "Eureka, eureka, for it works like a charm!" He called it "The American Flying Machine". The Wright brothers were 5 and 10 years old when Charlie Cowan, a hired hand on Murrell's farm, made several flights of several hundred yards before a patent was awarded on August the fourteenth, in eighteen hundred and seventy four. It was the first, "heavier than air flying machine" registered in the United States of America.

YOU KNOW, THERE WERE MANY THINGS GOING ON AROUND MY HOMEPLACE. THANKS, OAK TREE! THANKS FOR POINTING OUT ALL THESE THINGS THAT SURELY MAKE ME PROUD TO HAIL FROM HAMBLEN COUNTY, TENNESSEE.

What did you say, mister?

I, UH! OH! UH, GOOD MORNING SIR! I UH, WAS JUST TALKING TO MYSELF ABOUT HOW NICE THIS OLD OAK TREE IS. IT MUST HAVE BEEN HERE A LONG TIME. A LOT OF HISTORY HAPPENED UNDER THIS TREE.

Yep! Sure is. I hear they're going to remove it, along with some others to make room for a kind of gazebo, here by the spring.

NOT IF I CAN HELP IT, THEY'RE NOT! NOT IF I CAN HELP IT!

You come from around here do you?

SURE DO! WHY, I WAS BORN RIGHT OVER THERE ON THE OTHER SIDE OF THAT MOUNTAIN. YES SIR, THIS IS MY HOME. THIS IS MY HOME!

Peace of Mind

Peace is an original feeling of contentment in the mind of man
that properly expires at the age of accountability
and becomes his temporary refuge, an untenable haven, for all subsequent thought.
Without original peace, he would have no knowledge of where his mind can go,
if 'twere lasting peace, he would have no need to travel there.

The Moon of Gethsemane

I saw the moon last night and remembered Christ's Prayer.
He prayed in the Garden of Gethsemane that His Father would change His mind.
Yet, His death did come to pass, and in a most hideous way, so as to emphasize
His ultimate payment for the forgiveness of the sins of The Children of God.

I saw the stars last night and thought of my young parents, long ago.
They carved a meager existence; however they could, as they spread joy to their children.
Yet, whatever they did, each individual child would walk a different direction in life
Toward a different goal as if they, like the stars, seemingly had no guidance whatsoever.

I saw darkness last night and wondered what my descendants would find in their lives.
Much philosophical turmoil exists in the world that will be waiting for them.
Although my parents must have pondered the same questions for their children,
It seems that my thoughts are more profoundly challenging for the times to come.

I looked at the sky today and watched, as the clouds went drifting by.
They pass over all the children of this earth who harbor the ideals of many minds.
Why then, can't we explore these thoughts to know how they can live together?
If I look to the heavens tonight, will I look upon my "Moon of Gethsemane"?

Summer Snows

'MORNIN' PRESCOTT,
"Guess it tiz!"
YA KNOW THAT CRAG UP TUH SMATHERS' FAHM?
"Lowah ah uppah,? There's two ya know!"
UPPAH!
Thayuz a lowah, too!
I SAID UPPAH, FOR GOD'S SAKE!
Well, ya didn't give me thu choice. Ya only said uppah when ah asked ya.
IT WAS THU UPPAH CRAG UP TUH SMATHER'S FAHM! IS THAT CLEAH ENOUGH?
"Ayuh, What about it? Haven't got all day. Shoein' this mule!""
WELL, THIS MAHNIN', AH NOTICED IT HELD UH BIT O'SNOW.
"So what's so strange about snow in Maine, Silah?
AH THOUGHT IT UH BIT STRANGE IN AUGUST?
"Old man Smathers' don't only seem uh bit strange, Silah, he's always been uh bit strange.
AH DIDN'T SAY SMATHERS WAS STRANGE, PRESCOT, AH WAS SPEAKIN' OF THU' SNOW.
"Ah heard ya Silah, and ah clearly asked ya what's s'peculiar 'bout uh little snow heah in Maine? Already told ya, old Smathers is more'n uh mite strange.
WELL, AH THOUGHT IT UH BIT STRANGE T'FIND SNOW ON THU UPPAH CRAG IN AUGUST, PRESCOTT.
"What more do ya expect me t'say about that crag, Silah?"
TRUTHFULLY, AH DIDN'T EXPECT MUCH MOAH THAN WHAT AHM GETTIN'. YA JUST GO ON SHOEING THAT MULE. YA NEVAH HAVE ANYTHING TO SAY THAT MEANS MUCH, ANYWAY.
"Now, just hold on Silah! Ya come in heah on this uncomfortable hot summah mornin'
n' start muh day by announcin' that ya saw thu uppah crag at Smathers' fahm an' ya say that it's me that don't say anything that means anything! Now, ahm tellin' ya that crag has been hanging off that mountain since Noah picked a pair o'mountain goats off it. Now, just what do ya want me t'say?"
AH THOUGHT YA MIGHT NOTICE THAT AH MANAGED THU' WORD "SNOW" INTO THE SENTENCE, PRESCOTT.

"Oh, ah noticed Silah, and ah thought it uh bit strange that ya mention snow in thu middle of summer but ya have been acting a little wobbly since ya spring cleanout. Ah warned ya, 'bout takin too much o'that stuff.

AH GIVE UP! AHM GOIN' OVER T'STORE. MAYBE SOMEONE THERE WILL HAVE MORE INTEREST.

"Ah doubt that, Silah, this is Old Smather's mule, Victoria, heard every word ya said, includin' thu insults. Ah worked thu woods with her all last summah and I got t'know her pretty good. Well, let me just tell ya, she don't take gossipin' lightly!

My Old Friend

There were only two occasions where I noticed that my best friend was severely crippled; the first time I saw him and the last time I saw him.

The Nettle

I can't determine if all our minds act the same. The study would be impossible, even if I wanted to find out, which I don't, really. But people must react the same to some situations and maybe even to some thought processes. I have some things that mean nothing to anyone, except me, that occurred in my youth that perhaps even scarred my mind; things that I think of in situations that happen now. One of those thoughts is of nettles.

Nettles are small plants, about a foot high, if I remember correctly, that are neither ugly nor pretty. Sometimes they have a yellow, marble-like berry that must be a seed bearer, as it looks like a fruit; again, neither ugly nor pretty, just there, like the rest of the plant. However, this plant is etched into my memory because of where and when it exists, its capabilities, and where it fits into my thoughts and most of all, philosophy of life.

Down in Dixie, nettles arrive in the hottest weather. They grow where land is washed out, such as on the banks of a ditch and usually in desolate, sandy, hot spots, where there are few other plants. Although they have what appear to be briar thorns, they not only prick, but also literally sting their victim, which often was me! In hot weather, this combination of assaults is especially irritating.

Southern kids put up with some pretty mean critters including snakes, hornets etc. I have sat in the hot sun for hours and watched "tumble-bugs" or "dung-beetles" roll balls of dung for great distances through great obstacles. Some of these things rate far below an "A" in daily entertainment, even to an eight-year-old farm boy, but they fascinated me. However, the nettle drove its picture home to be forever imprinted on my mind.

My home was on top of a hill and we had a footpath running straight down its face to join the road beside the pond. The pond was divided into three sections by a fence that continued through the water so that each field had a share for the cattle or horses. The road continued along the pasture fences, and the hill, to one of the tobacco-drying barns, and then along the top of the hill to the rear of the house. Foot traffic always used the shorter, although much steeper, path.

I had a small toy Caterpillar tractor with which I played in the dirt of the ditch. I knew very well the wrath of the nettle growing near me and did not touch it. I was playing there in the super-heat of a summer afternoon, when a wasp alighted on the nettle, thereby creating a picture that etched itself upon my brain for life. The reflected sun and the extremely hot afternoon heat burned down upon my skin and bare head. This pain, the ditch, where all the good soil had been washed away, the stinging weed and the wasp appeared in one uncomfortable picture of all things that are bad. The pure makings of hell!

At that moment, nothing was good! There was no promise of a cool, enriched tomorrow. I was left with only a hot and uncomfortable dead-end, within a minute empty wasteland, available to me. This, now philosophical, picture of the heat and the ditch, the stinging wasp and the nettle has never left my memory. I have never forgotten the sight, the threat, or the feeling.

During my life, I have seen many people with the look that I must have had that day. I have seen kids looking through the wire fence that separated us at the airports, thinking I'm sure, that they would never get to travel the world as I did. I also have seen old people with that same expression, while trying to manipulate their bodies into positions that, at a younger time, they had readily attained. I have seen it in news pictures of the hungry and the sick, and in pictures of prisoners of war. But most of all I see it on the faces of desolate children, perhaps because I was a child when I was captured by it and also felt desolate.

When I look at an object, I see something different than most people, I suppose. Because of my life's exposures, the same object probably means something different to me than to others, simply because we grew up differently. That alone is sufficient reason to respect each other's thoughts, isn't it?

The sleek airplane that I flew was a world away from the dirty kids hanging on the fence. I often wondered what they thought was contained inside my cockpit or what they thought I was thinking. Before the increased security concerns, I took many children aboard for a look when I had time. I wished that others would have, and could now do the same.

Philosophically, I try to keep in mind that there are many people, at any time, who are sitting in their ditch, looking at their nettle, and perhaps their wasp, or finding that the good soil has been removed from their life. We all have these moments at times. We just have to remember to stay away from the painful sting. And remember that even the "tumble-bugs" have a job that seems impossible, not very romantic, and the pay is not really that desirable, but they put all their heart into their task. I guess there's a lesson there, isn't there?

One night, my crew and I were preparing the aircraft for a trip from Boston to Florida when the Flight Attendant came forward and said "Captain, I have a gentleman who flew aircraft in World War I riding with us. Could he come to the cockpit, please?" I answered, "Yes, of course" and she led him in, totally wide-eyed and amazed at the hundreds of switches and meters glowing red in a darkened flight deck. I held a short conversation with him and then I had him sit in an observer's seat, directly behind me. The First Officer, the Second Officer and I continued with our duties and procedures. Occasionally, I had time to talk to him about his previous flight experiences. He had not been in an aircraft since 1918 when he was a pilot. We continued to complete our procedures as I taxied the aircraft about a mile to the take-off end of the runway where, by regulation, I had to ask the attendant to return him to his passenger seat. At this time, he asked, "When will you start the engines?" He couldn't hear the three engines, hundreds of times more powerful than the one he relied upon, already smoothly running, a hundred well-insulated feet behind us. He thought the tow-tractor had brought us to this point. While doing my normal operational duties, I had not thought of all the questions that he must have had. But then, I now know that I couldn't have, could I?

May There Always Be a Cloud in My Life

I remember many hot summer days when I spent some time lying under my mom's angel-hair fern that she kept on our front porch in Tennessee. It gave only partial shade like a veil but it smelled heavenly. I could look straight out at the wonderfully active cumulus clouds, constantly changing their shape over the Great Smoky Mountains and day dream. I could just let my mind ride the up-drafts with the turkey vultures. The mountains, the clouds, and the vulture, were all beautiful.

Later, my profession as an airline pilot would allow me to ride among such clouds on a daily basis. Sometimes I flew over them, sometimes below them, but I liked it most of all when they were cooperative enough to allow me the privilege of flying in and out of their wispy towers. I was always cognizant of their immense power and beauty, and in awe of what God had allowed me to do. They are a product of the moisture, temperature and the terrain working together to lift the moving air. At times, they would get grumpy and bumpy, and I would have to leave them to seek smoother air or slow the aircraft down, to reduce their lifting capabilities on my wings, softening the blow. However feisty, they were always beautiful. They are a perfect creation of Mother Nature.

When I die, I hope my Maker allows me to walk among them again. What a position that would be! The Herder of Cumuli, or H.C.! Did you ever see a good picture of a sunset without a cloud? Very few, I'll bet. There are, almost always, layers of clouds separating the wondrous array of colors caused by the rising or setting sun. During these times of day, the atmosphere is usually somewhat calm and the cumuli have changed to the flat strata shapes.

When I pass on to heaven, don't fret, because God leads the way, and He does no wrong. Of course, I'll do whatever He says, but I may just drop a hint that I'm available for the job.

Someone once related that the aviation profession is a full circle from beginning to end, because pilots begin, and usually retire to, the same type of small aircraft. I had known the story for years then, after retiring, I realized that I had not only completed the circle, but also had added a sailboat.

It began with a young man, sailing the sea in a tiny white sailboat. He looked upward, as a small aircraft flew over his head, and wished that he could fly an airplane, and look down on the ocean and his tiny craft.

That small aircraft's pilot was looking upwards at a corporate aircraft and wishing that he could fly one of those airplanes, taking important executives from city to city.

High above his craft streaked an airliner, which caused the corporate pilot to dream that someday, he would qualify to fly one of those gleaming beauties.

Meanwhile, the airline pilot was looking down through his cockpit side window thinking of tomorrow, his first day in retirement, when he would pull his little white sailboat out of his garage and be as the tiny dot he sees on the blue water miles below him.

Now, I have completed my circle and am now content to become the little white dot again, both practically and philosophically. I know that I will always miss the thrill of flight and will re-dream the dream that I was privileged to live, many times. I find absolute pleasure and peace now on the ocean, accompanied by dolphins, gulls and seals. I applaud when I see a whale, and I occasionally look up at an airplane, as I drink up more of the supreme wonders of God's Wonderful World, AMEN!

Where the Wind Whispers My Name

I have heard the phrase, "where the wind whispers my name", many times in reference to where you feel you belong. I understand the feelings of belonging and not belonging. I have such an experience in my life, but sometimes I am ashamed to think about it and seldom discuss it, especially with non-believers. Although I was always loved and cared for in an exemplary manner, I had feelings that I was somehow different. My siblings were always healthier and bigger at any age, and they just thought differently. I passed it off thinking everyone must think this way at times in his or her lives.

However, I felt it all too often and was ashamed of my feelings. No one had more caring and loving parents and siblings than I, and I certainly wouldn't want to know I was picked up in a trade somewhere. So, I just tried to ignore it.

Almost every doctor who ever examined me has asked if I was a multiple birth. Most point out some kind of malformation in the structure of my back and shoulders. But I always answered "no" and went on with my life. However, on the twelfth of March, 1953, when I called my mother to tell her that I was the father of a beautiful 11-pound, 12-ounce daughter, I learned of an event that verified my feelings. She had been especially worried that my wife, Marie would have a multiple birth because I had been born a triplet and the other two hadn't survived the birth.

Ultrasound was in the future and x-rays were not used on pregnant women. The doctor had told us that we would have twins or a very large baby. He was right! The excitement of the new baby was overwhelmingly joyous and, at the time, I didn't dwell on what my mother had told me. I think it really sank in my mind when, during my first flight physical, when the doctor asked the old question about multiple birth, I surprised myself by answering, "Yes, I was a triplet". His answer was short but, to me an ultra-profound "Uh huh!" with emphasis on the "huh!" Now I asked, and he explained my "differences" while he finished the physical. From that moment on, I felt I had changed for the better. I had found out more about myself and that is always good.

Mother passed away on Christmas Day, 1988. During my return to Tennessee, my brothers and son-in-law and I visited the family graves and my birthplace, near the Yellow Branch Church, in the Cumberland

Mountains. There, we met a gentleman who knew all the family and the relatives that are buried here. There were the graves of my grandparents Hurley, and some relatives, who were soldiers on both sides of the Civil War, and he had a story about each and every one of them. But there were two blank tomb "tablets" side by side and I asked him who they were because I had a strong, but unidentifiable, feeling about them. He said that he didn't know who they were, which I felt was very odd, indeed. I had a strong desire to know who was resting there.

I may be wrong but I feel that they are my brothers and I cannot change that feeling. In that small spot, I have a certain feeling of peace, well being and tranquility, that I find nowhere else. I cannot ignore it, nor do I wish to. The wind whispers my name there!

My Hobby-Quantum Physics

+++

{Author's note: I have included this excerpt from my thesis, originally entitled, "Infinite Creative Perfection", written of my thoughts on my personal spiritual/scientific theories in Creativity (or Intelligent Design), versus "Evolution". I believe that it is entirely proper to believe in both theories simultaneously. Indeed, it is impossible for me not to do so. Sometimes, theories are easier to understand than facts.}

+++

Come, relax and walk with me! Before we can understand one another we must get acquainted. Take a minute and look into my thought process. Every person has a thought base that is intentionally or unintentionally instilled by past events and surroundings, and personally modified by current events and surroundings. The word "duck" means one thing at the lake and another on the golf course! See what I mean? Yes, walk with me to a place we can escape the fantasyland in which we live, to a land where my mind finds peace, freedom and home!

I am totally fascinated by the theory of quantum physics. Where I grew up, in the mountains, distances can be confusing. Once, I stood in the Great Smoky Mountains, looking down on a farm far below, in a place called Maggie Valley. The farmer was feeding his beagles. Their barking sounds and his voice were carried so well, that it seemed that they were only a short distance away. But they were far enough that, by the time the sounds reached me, the movements were no longer coordinated with them. I saw the screen door to his porch shut a long while before I heard it. I experienced a, sometimes eerie, ghostly feeling that occurs when otherwise familiar actions and sounds are not coordinated, which brings me to the quantum thing.

I had seen the action of the door closing. It had happened! Yet, to my son standing beside me and looking elsewhere, this didn't happen until some time later when he heard the sound. To him, at precisely the moment when he heard the sound, the event occurred. So, when did it happen? When he heard it, or when I saw it? The same event had occurred at different times in our lives. I find that very interesting, especially when I look at different examples and effects.

On another occasion in the Cumberlands, a tractor, miles away, was moving around a herd of cattle. It was so far away that it was almost indistinguishable without binoculars. Without binoculars, the tractor simply did not exist in my life. But to the farmer driving that tractor and to the person watching with binoculars, it most certainly existed.

When a ship departs from port, just before it disappears over the horizon, it changes from a container of "flesh and blood life" to an inanimate object. It is difficult to look at the dot on the horizon and still hold the image of the live passengers in your mind.

Science tells us that some of the stars we see in the sky do not exist; that the stars burned out years ago, and that we are just seeing a continuation of the shaft of light that is still traveling toward us. This light was emitted when the star existed. The end of that shaft of light is also rushing toward us at the speed of light, but may take many more light years to reach us. When it does reach us, the star will cease to exist; i.e. it will cease to exist to the people who do not know that it has extinguished already. The star has already died to the scientist but not to our eyes.

Let's pretend, for a moment that we can stop time in its tracks and stop the back end of this shaft of light just as it gets on our side of the moon. This starlight shaft still can be seen, so the star still exists. Now, we focus our binoculars on a point just past the moon, past the back end of that light shaft. Now, there is no light from the star, so it no longer exists. We are now using binoculars to look into the future to what we will, or will not, be seeing, tomorrow, or our past, what has actually happened. Perhaps we are looking into the past because we know the star's demise has already happened and now can see the fact. So what is the difference between the past and the future? We can reduce the focus of the glasses until we see the light shaft again and return to the present. The difference in the past, present and the future gets a little fuzzy in quantum science. Keep your mind open and let's go one step further. You see either conclusion is correct, according to our approach to it, isn't it?

If we can see both past and future, then, with a more powerful binocular, we can look far enough to see quasars. Scientists say that the explosion that created quasars took place during the creation of the earth and the heavens. Quasars are the furthermost or first remnants of that explosion from which the earth was created, the "big bang" that scientists talk about! These quasars are still moving outward and, with the new space-borne radio telescopes, are studied more every day to try to find answers to our questions about the creation of the universe. Are you still with me?

These facts bring many profound thoughts and their resulting questions of what relation time has to space and enhanced vision. Because the speed of sound, at some 700 miles per hour, is more basic and easier to grasp than the speed of light, it is usually used as an example of this relationship. Time and light travel are many times faster and it is sometimes difficult, even for scientists, to comprehend. Until lately, it was thought that the speed of light was the maximum speed attainable. Now, in an experiment, within a study, called "quantum tunneling", neutrons have been accelerated to a speed 1.7 times the speed of light. So, then, does time travel at a definite speed? No one knows. In quantum science, the Laws of Probability always rule and no rules are permanent.

If we increase our binocular focus beyond quasars, will we see that which existed before the earth was born (the past), or where we are going (the future)? If we change our focus at the same speed as the quasars are moving outward from the big explosion, are we freezing time causing it to stand still? If we traveled at these speeds, would we stop aging? If we accelerate beyond that speed, will we become younger, or older? Wonderful, thought provoking questions!

Either an increase or a decrease of our speed through space could be catastrophic. In fact, some scientists say that another world may be milliseconds behind or ahead of us, traveling through time at the same speed as we are. Einstein questioned it, and so did Sagan! Are there people who have been joggled out of the time groove, in which we all travel, by just a tad? For some reason my wife thinks so. That may explain gifted people, geniuses or, in my case, retarded minds, or even how the mind gets into the body. Doesn't the Bible mention that we are known before we are conceived? And what about ghosts, visions, spirits, haunted places and what about death? What about the rocks and the tree (that doesn't exist) that my friend and I saw when lost in the sea fog? Were we simply moved out of our groove? Is time only a thought process? Again, Einstein and Sagan pondered that question.

If we just let our minds go, unrestrained, let them explore what has been, what is, and what could be, we would enjoy more of our lives. There is plenty to enjoy. Don't get tied into thinking anything is concrete. In 1760, a man named Thomas Bayes came along with his "Theorem of Subjective Probability", which is a proposition that all minds have knowledge beyond their conscious recognition. In other words, our brain is smarter than we think it is. Of course, we could never explain the actions or mind of our Creator. He gave us an inquiring mind, a spirit and knowledge enough to use it. He gave us unlimited opportunity to improve it.

That's my story of the mind that I believe God has given to you and to me. I used to think that anyone who strayed from the wording of the Bible was being sacrilegious. However, I think He was far beyond patting clay with His hands in His creation of man and the universe. I believe that it was the way the record keepers and storytellers of our history illustrated it. In their language, they were exactly right and, no matter what I say or have said, I still believe the Bible is the inspired and true Word of God. But I believe that He has given me a thought process to better put it closer to reality for myself, and I give Him all the credit, for His Supreme Intelligence. I question why people try to rush the ending of God's earth by saying that it will end soon. God created this earth along with the heavens, over 15,000,000 light years ago. That's 13.7 billion calendar years. Christ was here only 2,000 years ago. That's not even a tenth of one light year. Remember the example that, if the calendar year represented the time that the earth has been in existence, we appeared at almost 11:30 PM on December 31st. I think it will be here for a while.

There is a sub-theory, if you will, called "Quantum Mechanics" that deals with energy matter that is smaller than an atom. The "quantum states" include physical properties of energy, motion and magnetic fields. There are many options, but quantum physics helps me to think that, just maybe, this world got here through creativity. Now, I am free to try to understand its relation to evolution or vice versa. I believe that evolution is simply a product, and certainly a process, of creativity. But nothing is created by chance.

Even when I was in school, I didn't like the "big bang" theory of evolution as a singular creative tool, because it disallowed an open and accommodating thought process. It seems to me that, although a tool, evolution is simply a credible "situation solution" that an already created body may involuntarily experience, but it certainly does not deserve "creative" status. It also seems to me that evolution is like discovering a reason "after the happening", like the explanation of stock market fluctuations. You can explain evolution to me and I'll say "Uh huh, Uh huh!" but when I study the quantum states, I say, "Oh, yeah!"

The easiest way for me to understand all this is to call on an old axiom called "contraction". To use it, imagine all the galaxies, planets, stars, quasars, earth and all their contents, including you and me, being thrown outwards with a horrific explosion, called the big bang! Now! Imagine this event occurring backwards. Trillions and trillions of pieces coming together, combining and shrinking back to the size of the earth, then to the size of a baseball, then an atom, then infinity. Got it? Everything's here in the dot! Now, let's re-live the explosion. BANG! Now freeze the action immediately and let's talk for a minute.

Scientists say that the explosion that started this universe, in order to have produced the results that were attained, had to have reached an accuracy of 10 to 15 decimals within seconds after the happening. That means that, within seconds, all the pieces necessary to form everything that now exists were irreversibly and perfectly assured. To me, that perfection fits God's creative talents to a "T".

Here are displayed the perfectly simplistic complexities of a Creator, a concrete concept of "perfect mathematical logic", Godly Logic over chance. A Perfect Creation, God's way.

In the beginning of this century/millennium, two astronomers, attempting to find microwaves in the galaxies, saw "static" on their screens. They decided that their find was caused by dirt in the antenna horn, which hadn't been cleaned in years. They proceeded to sweep and clean this horn and, after hours of labor, found that the "static" remained on their scopes. On further investigation, they realized that they had found exactly what they had been looking for, that it wasn't hiding as they had thought, and it wasn't dust. They had found that microwaves that started from the "big bang" still exist. The waves however, have been stretched back from the point where the quasars created by the "big bang" have traveled. We can tune our TV to a channel that is not used and see that "interference" on the screen. Some of the static is from local electrical interference but much of it is microwave energy from the explosive creation of the universe. Imagine! It is still visible and displayed right before our eyes.

Yes, imagine seeing radio waves and microwaves in our living room that were created when the galaxy we live in was created, 13.7 billion years ago. Scientists can now study these microwaves back, to within one second after the explosion. That sub-atom-sized object exploded to enormous quantities, leaving all the properties, elements and gasses necessary for life along the way.

There are exploding stars called super-novas that become many times hotter than the sun, with 4 billion times its energy, and create hydrogen, helium and oxygen. All the known life-supporting elements, down to the last element (iron), are found in the Milky Way. The galactic pictures of the Eagle Nebula that were recently taken by the Hubbell telescope, exposed enormous proportions of matter in the universe. One area appears to contain veil-like, vertical clouds consisting of "dust-like" particles near the tip. Those tiny looking particles are giant stars, many times larger and hotter than our sun. The elements of life are widespread. There are billions of life-friendly galaxies in the universe; oxygen and life-supporting elements are found light years away from earth.

Some of the testing equipment is expensive, as we know from the price and upkeep of Hubbell but, in contrast, to find the existence of the elements on any given star, light is collected and channeled through a simple panel of holes, onto a prism. Each element then projects as a different color emanating from the prism.

Scientists witness many "heavenly events" each year and fail to see many more. The single most powerful event that occurs in the universe is the phenomenon called "gamma ray bursts". These explosions can destroy complete galaxies. As the big bang created the universe, gamma ray bursts can cause the catastrophic extinction of all creation by, of all things, fire and brimstone (burn-stone). It is a perfectly predicted destruction of the perfect creation of a Perfect God. As the director of the Hayden Planetarium stated, "The big bang was certainly no accident." Neither will the destruction by accident.

This theory has shored up my beliefs in God and the view that the Bible is man's "Godly-Inspired" accounting of history. I therefore believe that anything was, and indeed is, possible within man's mind and soul and I am at peace with those beliefs. Nevertheless, animosity still abounds in the world about our origin, beliefs and religions.

There are those who question the happening of miracles and there are those who believe that lowly men can judge who will be a Saint. There are questions about the Resurrection and the Immaculate Conception. It is human nature I suppose, that everything the mind thinks it understands as good, is credited to Our God, while everything we dislike or do not understand is blamed on the devil. If the event that we disliked later turns out to be beneficial, it was God "working in mysterious ways." We tend to be flexible in our religions!

We also use our closed minds to judge the actions of our fellow man. I have known Catholics and Protestants who will not enter the other's church, yet they will utilize a gambling casino or strip club together. Prejudice toward a man's color is no more or less a sin than prejudice toward his beliefs. How can we not accept one who listens with an open mind and heart, and truly lives within his beliefs and conscience, no matter what they are? How can we expect him to act contrary to his true knowledge or what he truly believes that "his God" expects of him, however he was exposed to these beliefs?

Actions of animals are not plotted or planned. Animals instinctively react to all situations with the innocence that feels right for their survival. The way they conduct their life is based on the coordination of instinct and immediate need. With the added gifts of education, practical knowledge, faith and justice, so should man.

Columnist Charles Krauthammer wrote the following statements in his Washington Post article Entitled, "Phony Theory, False Conflict" About the latest "Intelligent Design" discussion: He said, "I feel obligated to point out what would otherwise be superfluous: that the two greatest scientists in the history of our species were Isaac Newton and Albert Einstein, and they were both religious." He said: "Newton's God was not at all so crude. The laws of his universe were so simple, so elegant, so economical and therefore so beautiful, that they could only be divine." He went on to say that, "Neither saw science as an enemy of religion".

Mr. Krauthammer concluded: "How ridiculous to make evolution the enemy of God. What could be more eloquent, more simple, more brilliant, more economical, more creative, indeed more divine, than a planet with millions of life forms, distinct and yet, interactive, all ultimately derived from accumulated variations in a single double stranded molecule, pliable and fecund enough to give us mollusks and mice, Newton and Einstein? Even if it did give us the Kansas State Board of Education, too."

I wholeheartedly agree! I hope you have enjoyed our talk. So Long! CDH

+++

{AN ACTUAL LETTER FROM MY FRIEND, CODY}

+++

Radiogram
To: The Hurleys
On Board R*M*S "TITANIC"
Apr 14,1912

Hi folks- Just left South Hampton England.

Had dinner at Captain Smith's table. What a magnificent ship she is! What class and she's un-sinkable, imagine!

The Wideners & the Astors were asking for you, also Bador Straus & his wife, (and Ira Guggenheim).

Please have my private train stand by in New York. Anxious to see you!
Love, Cody.

P.S. The mate tells me we are entering the Northern Ice Floes in 27 hours or so! Ah, but she's unsinkable!

We are making great time so will arrive New York on schedule...........*C*